The
Library
of World
Biography

Chaplin

by Roger Manvell, *1909—*

ILLUSTRATED

THE LIBRARY OF WORLD BIOGRAPHY

J. H. PLUMB, GENERAL EDITOR

Little, Brown and Company — Boston – Toronto

COPYRIGHT © 1974 BY ROGER MANVELL

ALL RIGHTS RESERVED. NO PART OF THIS BOOK MAY BE REPRO-
DUCED IN ANY FORM OR BY ANY ELECTRONIC OR MECHANICAL
MEANS INCLUDING INFORMATION STORAGE AND RETRIEVAL SYS-
TEMS WITHOUT PERMISSION IN WRITING FROM THE PUBLISHER,
EXCEPT BY A REVIEWER WHO MAY QUOTE BRIEF PASSAGES IN
A REVIEW.

FIRST EDITION

T 11/74

LIBRARY OF CONGRESS CATALOGING IN PUBLICATION DATA

Manvell, Roger, 1909–
    Chaplin, by, Roger Manvell. ③ Boston, Little, Brown
    [1973] ix, 240 p, illns. 21 cm. ③
    (Library of world biography)
    Bibliography: p. [227] - 230.
    1. Chaplin, Charles, 1889– ② I, t
    PN2287.C5M28   791.43'028'0924 [B]   74-13119
    ISBN 0-316-54550-3

Published simultaneously in Canada
by Little, Brown & Company (Canada) Limited

PRINTED IN THE UNITED STATES OF AMERICA

Introduction

WHEN WE LOOK BACK at the past nothing, perhaps, fascinates us so much as the fate of individual men and women. The greatest of these seem to give a new direction to history, to mold the social forces of their time and create a new image, or open up vistas that humbler men and women never imagined. An investigation of the interplay of human temperament with social and cultural forces is one of the most complex yet beguiling studies a historian can make; men molded by time, and time molded by men. It would seem that to achieve greatness both the temperament and the moment must fit like a key into a complex lock. Or rather a master key, for the very greatest of men and women resonate in ages distant to their own. Later generations may make new images of them — one has only to think what succeeding generations of Frenchmen have made of Napoleon, or Americans of Benjamin Franklin — but this only happens because some men change the course of history and stain it with their own ambitions, desires, creations or hopes of a magnitude that embraces future generations like a miasma. This is particularly true of the great figures of religion, of politics, of war. The great creative spirits, however, are used by subsequent generations in a reverse manner — men and women go to them to seek hope or solace, or to confirm despair, reinterpreting the works of imagination or wisdom to ease them in their own desperate necessities, to beguile them with a sense of beauty or merely to draw from them strength and understanding. So this series of biographies tries in lucid, vivid, and dramatic narratives to explain the greatness of men and women, not only how they managed to secure their niche in the great pantheon of Time, but also why they have continued to fascinate subsequent generations. It may seem, therefore, that it is paradoxical for this series to contain living men and women, as well as the dead, but it is not so. We can recognize, in our own time, particularly in those whose careers are getting close to their final hours, men and women of indisputable greatness, whose position in history is secure, and about whom the legends and myths are beginning to sprout — for all great men and women become legends, all become in history larger than their own lives.

Men of action know their destiny. Alexander, Charlemagne, Louis XIV, Napoleon, Lenin, Hitler, and scores and scores of others who have been both the scourges and the molders of mankind are aware in their own lifetime that they will live in recorded history. Artists are a different matter. Some, like Horace, boast that their works will outlive monuments of bronze, and achieve their boast, but for the majority who write or paint or compose, their destiny remains hope rather than certainty. This is even more true of actors. And one wonders if the possibility could have ever crossed the mind of the first players in film. Money, yes; but immortality, I expect few gave it a thought. And perhaps it was as well they did not, for their eyes almost certainly would have been cocked on the immortals of the established theatre and so missed the new vistas that film made possible.

Of all the great figures, and there are many, that the

cinema has produced, Charles Chaplin is the most certain of immortality. He had the luck, as all great artists must have, to be in the heroic age of a new art. Would all of Shakespeare's plays be snapped up, unrevised by a modern producer? Would the editor of any publisher accept uncut the sprawling novels of Dostoevski? To be at the beginning of a new art, or to be present in a sudden new direction of an old art, is an inestimable advantage for a gifted man.

Chaplin, doubtless, would have made both a name and a fortune as a comedian in the theatre for his technical gifts — timing, mime, and physical control, all near perfection, and his emotional range, his capacity to infuse comedy with a tragic sense, and tragedy with a touch of farce would always have added the quality of genius to his technical gifts. But film increased the physical dimensions in which he could operate — giving possibilities for clowning and for pathos totally outside the range of the theatre, and also an audience of a magnitude never before dreamed of by an actor. An actor may, on occasion, act to tens of thousands over a long run, but none, not even the greatest, could ever hope to reach tens of millions. And this Chaplin has done. Such a triumph is epic. And epic in its true sense. Epics last because they touch the deep chords of human hope and fear; stir the mysteries of human life: the capacity to suffer, to endure, to accept. And Chaplin, the tragicomic victim of men and circumstances, the perpetual outsider, was both deeply original and the heir of a great tradition. The tradition was that of the great clowns, going back to Harlequin and beyond. But the originality lay in Chaplin's capacity to focus his art on the social stresses of his day, so that millions could identify, laugh at, and at times weep at their own plight which he symbolized.

The late nineteenth and early twentieth century witnessed an astonishing migration of people. From the east of Europe and from the south, families began to move west to the great developing industrial regions. America, particularly the eastern regions and the mining areas, was flooded with immigrants, but America was not alone. England absorbed in the East End of London, in Manchester, Bradford and elsewhere, large contingents of Russian and Polish Jews, as well as many Italians from the south. The French mining areas absorbed Poles, and so did those in Belgium. Rarely, perhaps never in the history of mankind, have so many families uprooted themselves to settle in a new environment that both beckoned and menaced. At the best these migrants possessed only a scrappy knowledge of the language of their new countries, sometimes not even that. They were often ignorant of the forces of authority with which they had to contend, or even their own rights under the law. They all had the potential to be silent victims — unable to communicate articulately with those who bullied and suppressed them. The alien immigrants' plight was only the extreme form of the plight in which the poor and the lower middle class had always found themselves — semiliterate, possessors of an impoverished vocabulary, intimidated by the rules and regulations of authority, they, too, were often the voiceless victims of society. Both aliens and the native poor had been thrust into new and alarming environments by rapid urbanization and industrialization; hence when Chaplin began to make films he had a vast and natural audience who could identify with his acute helplessness and with his rubber-like endurance and his poverty-driven cunning. And, of course, it was completely right that his films should be silent. Language, to the classes that he touched, was often baffling and difficult, and even more important, his art could sail with ease across national frontiers. The world was his audience.

Perhaps, however, the most miraculous factor of Chaplin's art is the way in which it grew ever more sophisticated, yet always keeping in step with the development of his mass audience.

One of the great unsung triumphs, not only of America but also of Europe, in the twentieth century has been the education of their masses. Billions of men and women have become not only literate but also aware of the world beyond their communities, of its problems and complexities. Their knowledge of geography, history, rudimentary science, primitive though it may be, is incomparably greater than ever before known in the history of mankind. This education of the masses is frequently ignored, and when not ignored, derided. Chaplin was instinctively aware, as indeed were many of the more creative men and women in the world of film, of this sophistication of the audience, and so his films steadily became more complex, more subtle, more penetrating in social criticism. One has only to compare *The Kid* or *The Gold Rush* with *Modern Times* or *Monsieur Verdoux* to realize the distance that not only Chaplin had covered, but also his mass audience.

What no one can deny is that Chaplin is a major figure in the popular culture of the twentieth century, a figure, indeed, already becoming mythic, and therefore deserving of a place in this library of world biography.

J. H. PLUMB

Contents

Illustrations

❦

Chaplin

❦

ONE

Charlie
A Twentieth-Century Legend

CHARLIE CHAPLIN is a Cinderella of the twentieth century. He embodies the wish fulfillment of our time, the boy who rose from the rags of Kennington to the riches of Hollywood. Others have paralleled this form of phenomenal success, inside and outside Hollywood, indeed in most parts of the world where the self-made rise to wealth. But Charlie is unique because he created a universal image on the screen with whom everyone among the millions who responded to his films could in some measure identify — the "little fella," penniless but resourceful; the vagabond with the gift of dreams; the poet of love, though of a love which more often than not remains unfulfilled.

The "little fella," who was in so many respects a projection of Charlie himself, was also archetypal man, perhaps already a little old-fashioned by the 1920s in his gallantry to the girls, long-suffering but always capable of delivering a subtly timed back kick at his oppressors, a man of courage who nevertheless knew when it was best policy to run away. He aspired, like every man, to possess his own little home, but more often than not he had to abandon such dreams and wander off toward the horizon with a jaunty swing of his cane. He was a tramp, but a tramp with a middle-class background and culture. His clothes were the battered remnants of middle-class respectability, and his manners, when he showed them, were those of the city man who likes to cut a dash even though the means of paying for it as often as not fall through the hole in the pocket of his pants. He was exposed to the overbearing authority of store-keepers, waiters, landlords and cops. But there seemed to be no place, however elevated, Charlie could not enter with his natural panache, and no environment from which in the end he would not finally be chased out. But the vagabond was always blended with the man-about-town, the rogue with the gallant, the waddling clown with the graceful acrobat and balletic mime, the poet with the simple day-dreamer. He was to blend melancholy with humor, his aspirations fading unfulfilled. He put the realities of poverty, starvation and violence on the screen as unfailingly as Dickens had put them into his novels. His evident vul-nerability appealed to the protective instinct in women, while the artist in him excited their romantic fantasies, just as Pierrot had come to do in the theater of the eighteenth and nineteenth centuries.

All this, and much else which any generalized description of Charlie's art must inevitably fail to convey, contributed to create recognition on a world scale which could not have existed in any previous century, and has not been equaled yet in this one. Charlie was to be as astonished as everyone else in the 1920s at the phenomenal reaction he had aroused. After all, he was only an entertainer, a comic mime, who had been a well-established young professional comedian on the stage in 1913. But by 1920 he had become a world figure and a millionaire because he had taken the step, uncertainly at first, of going on the screen.

He was lucky in the timing of his debut. The medium

was new and waiting its full development. The period —
that of the First World War — was a melancholy one in dire
need of cheap and heartwarming entertainment. Charlie
had, in effect, no real rivals once he had sensed the capa-
bilities of the silent film and stretched his talents to meet
them. It was "open sesame." There were other fine clowns.
There were other fine stars. But Charlie in a bare two years'
hard work had swept to the forefront of them all, and
offered new qualities of comic entertainment to which the
world was only too ready to respond.

It was a case of incredible talent coinciding with incredible luck and incredible timing. All this combined to give
him the success which has made him the archetypal star, the
single most famous man in the world of twentieth-century
entertainment.

When Charlie edged nervously into Mack Sennett's Keystone Studios late in 1913, wondering if he had done the
right thing to leave the stage on which his foothold was
assured, and accept the somewhat larger salary the untried
medium offered him, the silent film was less than twenty
years old. It had been the cumulative invention of a number
of countries — in the forefront, the United States, Britain,
France, and Germany. It was an extension of still photography, which had of course been familiar to the public since
the middle years of the nineteenth century. But it was not
until 1896 that audiences had enjoyed the opportunity to
familiarize themselves with an entirely new medium of
entertainment — a moving photographic image projected
onto a screen, and capable of recording scenes from life, real
or enacted, for some minutes on end.

The earliest films, lasting until well into the first years of
the twentieth century, were all short in duration, and covered every kind of subject likely to attract an audience for

a brief while — news items, travelogues, "interest" films on general topics (the primitive ancestors of documentary), little dramas and comedies with mimed action, trick films exploiting camera devices (such as reverse motion or speeded-up action), and living portraits in motion (but not yet with sound) of vaudeville artists, including popular singers and comedians. It had been the hope of Edison and of others who had pioneered motion picture photography and projection that one day sound recording could be directly linked with motion pictures. The rapid, parallel development of the phonograph, later the Gramophone, encouraged this hope, but the problem of amplification for sizable audiences as well as the quality of the sound itself were to frustrate this until the 1920s. Hence Charlie became a pioneer of the silent cinema, with which his art was to be essentially linked.

The earliest filmmakers at the turn of the century were gradually beginning to grasp the difference between a motion picture show and the popular magic-lantern entertainments of the nineteenth century. Magic-lantern "lecture" shows, with a *compère* or narrator, would take an audience through the phases of a story projected onto the screen in a series of still pictures. There was a tradition in art for this going back to ancient times, successive pictures or reliefs which portrayed the key moments in the development of a story. The first films were much like this in form and continuity — with the important addition that the pictures moved.

The early pioneer films were a series of single-shot scenes, a dozen or so for a five- or six-minute story, the camera statically and stolidly recording each successive scene. The progression from this to a freer, more fluid style of storytelling, breaking up the action into smaller segments and editing, or composing it into a more exciting flow of pictures gradually becoming more responsive to the movements of the actors, was the work of pioneer directors such as Edwin S. Porter in the United States and Cecil Hepworth in Britain during the years following 1903.

Edwin S. Porter made his six-minute pioneer western, *The Great Train Robbery*, in this year, and he went so far as to use picturesque location shots set in woodlands, as well as putting the camera onto the tender of a railway engine in motion, and panning and tilting the camera during the actual recording of a shot in order to follow the movements of the bandits escaping through the woods. Such small developments as these, or that by Hepworth, who in 1905 set his camera close to the ground in his domestic drama about a dog, *Rescued by Rover*, were beginning to reveal the elementary potentialities of the motion picture camera as a medium which could play its own essential part in making an action exciting to watch, especially when successive images were varied to emphasize different aspects of the action and then assembled in such a way as to bring their own tempo to bear on the audience, increasing the physical impact of the action by the very way in which it was presented visually.

This developing sense of "film form," among many other things, had been the special contribution of the first genius of motion pictures, the American David Wark Griffith, during the years immediately preceding Charlie's arrival in films. Fourteen years older than Charlie, he had been born in 1875 in a village near Louisville, Kentucky. Griffith was the son of a tough-spirited Confederate officer, Colonel Jacob Wark Griffith, whose Kentucky mansion had been burned down in the first years of the Civil War, and who was a prominent officer in the early Ku Klux Klan. His family, like Charlie's, had fallen on evil days, and he had stopped working on the family farm and become a shop assistant in Louisville, where he had seen his first theatrical performances. He had disgraced the family by going on the stage at the age of seventeen.

Griffith, who was to become a friend and business associate of Charlie, had experienced in youth, as Charlie had in childhood, penury, hunger, and the life of the hobo, while starving between engagements in stock during the 1890s. He had tried to keep a toehold on the stage as he eked out an existence in the flophouses of New York, or helped man the lumber schooners of San Francisco. He had lived as a laborer and occasional actor until 1907, supplementing his sparse earnings by gaining a few dollars through writing. He had by now a wife to support, Linda Arvidson, whom he had married in 1906. In 1907 he was suddenly dazzled when Jerome K. Hackett, the theatrical impresario, gave him one thousand dollars for a play called *The Fool and the Girl*. He also began to earn a few dollars writing scenarios for the Biograph Film Company of New York, for which he also occasionally acted at the rate of five dollars a day; the man who directed him was Edwin S. Porter. By June 1908 he had begun his career as a film director, making *The Adventures of Dollie* in two days at a production cost of sixty-five dollars. Among the people he was to hire as actors was a "strong man" from Canada, a onetime boiler-maker called Mack Sennett, who joined Biograph in 1909. Sennett became the company's slapstick comedian. Only four years later Sennett was to take charge of his own company, Keystone, out in California, and make history by hiring Charlie and introducing him to the screen.

Progress in the American cinema largely centered around Griffith for some years following 1908. His contribution to narrative and dramatic filmmaking included almost everything that constituted the idiom of the art. Not only did he give it form and structure, he brought it scale and dimension. In the four hundred and more films he made between

1908 and 1914, the year he made his great three-hour epic, *The Birth of a Nation,* he put into full dramatic use the cut-in close shot, breaking up scenes and camera setups of varying distance to emphasize now the full group, now the telling detail; he used distance shots, bringing the grandeur and perspective of landscape to the medium, which had tended to be confined to stagelike sets and the very modest use of location. He intercut for suspense, as in the standard situation of those in need of rescue with the rescuers on the way; this, sometimes called parallel action, he liked to say had been suggested to him by continuities in Whitman's poems and Dickens's novels — a point the Russian film-maker Sergei Eisenstein was later to endorse in his published lectures and essays, *Film Form.* With the aid of his devoted cameraman, Billy Bitzer, Griffith experimented with photographic effects, with tinted stock associating mood with allover, monochromatic color effects (such as blue for night), as well as special lighting effects (such as those in Rembrandt's pictures, which Griffith studied in the New York art galleries, with their strong use of light and shadow, molding and dramatizing the characters' faces). He even shot directly into the sun to achieve effects of halation.

Griffith helped to move toward the feature-length films of the future by making *The Massacre* (1912; length: half an hour) and, above all, *Judith of Bethulia* (1913; length: one hour), though the vast majority of his films remained one-reelers, that is, fifteen-minute stories. In these he introduced to the screen new, largely untried and youthful players, including many who were to achieve fame in his films and the films of other directors; they included the Gish sisters, Mary Pickford, Mae Marsh, Wallace Reid, Henry Walthal, and later Walter Huston, W. C. Fields, and Tyrone Power, as well as Mabel Normand and Mack Sennett, who were to give Charlie his groundings in the new art of the cinema. Griffith even directed Mack Sennett in slapstick, though he was never to be noted as a comedy director.

The strong impulse behind Griffith's work was toward giving the "flickers" dignity, a status approaching that of the theater and dramatic literature. His cultural interests were steeped in the nineteenth century; his father had loved to declaim Shakespeare, and his own leanings were towards Dickens and (less known to his family) the rather less respectable poetry of Walt Whitman. His ancestral sympathies were with the South in the Civil War, as *The Birth of a Nation* was to show, and there can be no doubt that Griffith's severe limitations as an artist were that he brought to the cinema a traditional, nineteenth-century outlook which he somehow managed to combine with a wholly twentieth-century technical grasp of an entirely new medium, in all respects alien to the nineteenth century. He was also a pronounced Anglophile, which scarcely suited a largely isolationist America. Charlie himself, in spite of being fourteen years younger, was not entirely to escape from the social and human values of the nineteenth century, though he was only an adolescent when Queen Victoria died. Sennett, the farm boy from Canada, was to be quite free from such cultural and literary ties. But for Charlie, as for Griffith, the work of Dickens represented a profound influence. Both Griffith and Charlie entered the cinema unwillingly for the sake of the money and the potential fame it offered young men of talent, and they felt instinctively that they must raise it to their level if they were to continue to work in it to their own satisfaction.

This two-way pull, the total acceptance of the film's "vulgarity" of origin and its appeal to the basic entertainment needs of people uncluttered by middle-class "culture" and the "refinement" which many filmmakers tried to impose on the new medium, is an interesting reflection of the prewar period of production into which Charlie was to be thrust. In Italy, the *film dell'arte* movement was already bringing, or attempting to bring, D'Annunzio onto the screen (some twenty-five thousand dollars was paid in 1911 for the screen rights to his total work); in France, the *film d'art* movement was introducing the formal gestures, amplified into exaggerated mime, of the great actors and actresses of the Comédie Française onto the screen. There was a similar, less organized movement in Britain, resulting, for example, in Sir Johnston Forbes-Robertson's stage production of *Hamlet* being produced by Cecil Hepworth as a feature-length film in 1913. These were all interesting experiments, but they did not develop from the ground roots of the movie, which belonged more nearly to the fairground, vaudeville and burlesque, where, after all, the early films were for the most part to be shown. The full-time movie theaters (often converted vaudeville houses, burlesque theaters, and even restaurants) began to be established gradually after 1905, and with great rapidity after 1910, when the longer, feature-length movies were making their initial, tentative appearance, produced at first in Europe rather than in the United States.

Griffith was saved from such literary and theatrical excesses as the European art film movements normally represented by his own roots and background. He liked literature, but he had also been a Kentucky farmer's son, a Louisville salesman, a San Francisco sailor, a New York hobo, a migrant actor in stock. He did not forget that he must entertain the kind of people he knew best when making his movies, or lose eventually his fifty dollars a week. His aspirations were for himself and his new medium, to get the best he could out of the stories he chose to tell, which often came from literary sources. If he passed on little of this to Mack Sennett, Charlie would certainly understand what Griffith was striving to do in the cinema. When

Charlie entered the industry in December 1913, Griffith was planning, and striving to finance, his great independent production of *The Birth of a Nation,* which cost some $110,000, a phenomenal sum for the time. Biograph had grumbled severely when *Judith of Bethulia,* made the same year and running an hour, had cost them $13,000. But Griffith had at least taught Sennett to go for quality in his more considered films — some of the shorter ones were just improvised on the spot — and spend more money on quality players than Biograph had been prepared to do.

One other factor in the cinema must be mentioned to keep Charlie's future work in perspective. Certain "name" comedians were setting standards as comic personalities who appeared recurrently in films until they became favorites with the public, often to some extent outside their own countries. Among these was the French comedian, André Deed, known as Foolshead, whose major success was achieved in Italy. The most influential was another Frenchman, Max Linder, whose short comedies, scripted and directed by himself, had begun as early as 1907, and numbered almost a hundred by 1916. His work is therefore parallel to that of Griffith, and was more farcical in nature than violent slapstick. Like Charlie, he had worked initially on the stage, and understood how to time the comic business he devised for his films years before either Mack Sennett or Charlie were in the business on their own. Max Linder set unique standards which belonged to the same area as the comic sketches in which Charlie was appearing; both specialized in playing the drunk-but-dignified man-about-town, Linder on the screen and Charlie on the stage. Max Linder was an elegant, unruffled comedian, urbane and within his own limited style, sophisticated. Charlie, more than Mack Sennett (who was later to try unsuccessfully to employ Linder in Hollywood), was to learn something from Linder's films. Linder's achievement, coming as early as it did, was a notable step in refining alike the content of the short film sketches and the detail in their acting.

Charlie, therefore, was most fortunate in the timing of his arrival in the cinema. The first, difficult phase in the pioneer period was over, and a vast public was already being drawn to their local cinemas as regular weekly patrons. This public was to grow both in Europe and America during the war years, with the special need for cheap and easily available entertainment. Success on an unprecedented scale was waiting on talent. Griffith was shocked into awareness of this when he discovered, while still earning only fifty dollars a week, that Biograph was quietly making 1,700 percent annual profit on their investment in production. Although he was their leading director, and by far the best known in the business, they were still shortsighted enough to let him go when he asked for some reasonable percentage of the profits from his films. Plainly, this was just the period, 1913–14, for the independent artist to take risks and make money for himself by sharing — in one form or another — in the profits from his work. Mack Sennett had demonstrated this himself in 1912 by going into the business on his own account as producer and director.

There were other — social — factors which made this a good period in which to start a new career in films. The First World War, which was to commence in Europe within six months of Charlie's debut on the screen, was a watershed in the developing social attitudes of the greater mass of the people. It was to be the catalyst for a new society. The war in Europe, and later as it affected the United States, cut like a knife through the complacencies of the Victorian and Edwardian eras, and gave an entirely new slant to social values which had seemed to many, if not to most people, impregnable. By the time the war was over, after five catastrophic years, ancient monarchies had foundered, the central European map had been largely redrawn, the Soviet Union had set up an entirely new, so-called "people's state," Germany had been at least threatened by Communism, while America's isolationism had been largely disrupted and the global structure of the British Empire had begun to show the first signs that it might not last forever. Disillusion spread throughout the disaffected world, and fascist regimes established themselves, first in Italy, and then, within a decade, in Germany and Japan. There were economic depression and mass unemployment. The age began to be called that of the "common man" — meaning, presumably, that ordinary people, the so-called man and woman in the street, were potentially of equal value and interest as human beings to the members of the narrow society of the upper class, the titled people and the rich whose activities, real or fictitious, had dominated the popular stage, novel and screen. The cinema by the 1920s had become an established form of bourgeois as well as working-class entertainment.

The years of Charlie's greatest and most consistent success, from 1914 to 1940, were therefore those of the First World War and the years of the deeply disturbed interwar period which followed. This naturally was not to be without significance. His wit and his humanity, and all that it implied, spoke for this period, and it was not for nothing that Charlie's screen character was that of a gentlemanly tramp for whom dire poverty was to be a recurrent experience treated with considerable realism. Meanwhile, the world knew that Charlie himself had grown richer and richer, and indeed so famous that there was surely no one in civilized society who did not know his name. His regular patrons in the world's cinemas could be numbered in hundreds of millions.

This, too, was the "jazz age," the age in which many indulged in reckless, even lawless enjoyment, the age of the bootlegger and the gangster in the United States, the age of permissive reading, of the increasing recognition of the revolution in sexual and other values implicit in the work of D. H. Lawrence and James Joyce, and the popularization of the ideas of Havelock Ellis and Sigmund Freud. In the visual arts it was the age of cubism, of dada, of surrealism, of wildly experimental techniques in the theater, though these things touched the general public far less, and had little or no effect on the work of such universally recognized artists as Charlie. But it was an age in which risks could be taken in the arts, and Charlie took them, sometimes forfeiting the support of his public when he did so. For example, he risked writing and directing a serious, psychologically realistic film in *A Woman of Paris,* and he risked later making and starring in all-but-serious films in the case of *City Lights* and (above all) *Monsieur Verdoux,* as well as making all-but-silent films well into the sound era — up to and including *Modern Times* in 1936.

Public taste in the age he was serving changed and expanded with an increasing rapidity, while Charlie himself, an innately conservative person, had to take care during the 1930s that he was not being outmoded or left behind, like the great social writers he had come to know personally, Bernard Shaw and H. G. Wells. Shaw and Wells were respectively thirty-three and twenty-three years senior to him, and he could see how they insisted on propounding views in their old age to which their public had become overaccustomed. By the 1940s they were increasingly regarded as prophets and thinkers whom the times had largely overtaken. These were the dangers of too much fame, and too inflexible a dedication to an unchanging viewpoint in an age of shifting values and political unrest.

Charlie's career in motion pictures came, therefore, at the dawn of a new concept in entertainment — world stardom based not on the personal appearance of the artist at home or on tour, but on a reproduced image, copies of which could be indefinitely multiplied and exhibited any place where projection facilities were commercially available. The potentialities of this form of stardom had only begun to dawn on the film industry during the period Charlie entered it.

Stardom in the theater had, of course, been traditionally recognized for centuries. The Greek and Roman theaters had built up their star performers, whose individual work was recognized and acclaimed, and professional actors went on tour so that their talents were known in many widely spaced cities where their language was understood. Professional star actors appeared again during the sixteenth century in Europe, while in Japan the Noh and Kabuki forms of stylized acting demanded the highest skills from their noted practitioners. In England, Marlowe's plays were written to display the great talents of Edward Alleyn, his star performer, while Richard Burbage had the unique honor of introducing Shakespeare's tragic heroes to the Elizabethan public. The recognized companies of Elizabethan England toured not only Britain but the European continent, and stardom therefore became to a limited extent international.

Professional actresses appeared comparatively late on the English stage (around 1660), having begun their careers on the European continent the previous century. Up to this time, acting of any status had been entirely in the hands of men, who simulated women (with or without masks), most notably in the classical Greek drama and the Japanese Noh and Kabuki theaters, as well as in the drama of Elizabethan and Jacobean England, that is up to the closure of the theaters by the Puritan Commonwealth regime in 1648.

It is difficult to think of parts offering such great opportunities to women as Lady Macbeth, Queen Katherine,

Juliet, Rosalind, Cordelia, and above all Cleopatra being played by boys or young men. The brilliance of the female impersonation by contemporary male performers in Noh and Kabuki is perhaps a cue to this very special form of stardom. Charlie himself was later to perform brilliantly as a woman in his film for Essanay, *Charlie the Perfect Lady* (initially called simply, *A Woman*). He could no doubt have been highly successful in women's parts had he lived in Elizabethan England, and this entirely without the quality of "effeminacy" to which Colley Cibber referred.

However, the fame of great actors, the stars of the theater, was normally limited to their own countries until the nineteenth century — though Garrick, for example, paid a prolonged visit to France as a celebrity of the theater to study production methods in that country, while French and Italian companies visited England on occasion as early as the seventeenth century. The exception, very naturally, was America during and immediately after the colonial period. During the eighteenth century players began to brave the Atlantic crossing to bring drama from England, building up fresh reputations in the cities of the New World and earning for themselves additional money. But, in effect, star players did not develop in the theater of the United States or come from England to present seasons of plays until the beginning of the nineteenth century. Nevertheless, there were talented players working in the American theater somewhat earlier than this. Such were the Lewis Hallam company of 1752, John Hodgkinson, who arrived in America from Britain in 1792, and George Frederick Cooke, who came at the beginning of the nineteenth century. Hallam had emigrated from England and received enthusiastic support from George Washington, though there was much hostility to the theater among those Americans who had a strong Puritan strain in them. Cooke certainly had a talent with real star quality, though he was unfortunately addicted to drink, a common failing among players, as Charlie was to find out.

But it was the nineteenth century which saw the common recognition of stardom in America's links with Europe. During this period the Booth family moved to the United States, and Edwin Booth was to become one of America's greatest stars of the century, taking his place in the growing two-way traffic which carried him to England just as the English stars Edmund Kean, William Macready and Henry Irving made repeated tours in the United States. It was this tradition of sending established companies of leading players across the Atlantic which was to bring Charlie himself to America in the Karno company of comedians, first in 1910 and again in 1912, when he was finally to settle in the United States.

Stardom, therefore, as it was understood in the period virtually up to the First World War was a matter of fame created by the followers of the legitimate theater, who were necessarily a middle-class and upper-class elite of their own, or created in the burlesque or vaudeville theaters, which was stardom as it was understood by the working class, who loved their ballad singers, comedians, sketch players and raconteurs with a devotion equal to that the upper classes lavished on a Booth, an Irving, or an Ellen Terry. In all events, it was a personal contact, based on personal appearance and the "charisma" of the unique performance undertaken for that particular audience and no other. Irving's many tours of the United States were reported carefully in the London *Times,* recording the reception he was getting city by city, and one of his North American tours became the subject of a well-written and well-read book. But this could be said to be the limits of Irving's stardom as it was known in the nineteenth century — recognition by many in the streets of the cities where he was playing, and certainly in London, respect for his opinion in his clubs, enjoyment of the company of the eminent at the many parties he gave on stage at the Lyceum after the evening show. But Irving had virtually to ask for his knighthood, the first to be conferred upon an actor, whose social status, even as late as the 1890s, was still somewhat in doubt, in spite of the high position occupied in society by Garrick, John Philip Kemble and Sarah Siddons in the eighteenth century, followed by that of Macready, Irving and Terry in the nineteenth.

But after the cinema had been established for a decade or more, the nature of stardom underwent a complete change, working from ground level upward. Who, the public had begun to inquire by 1910, were those pretty but anonymous young girls who were seen so repeatedly in the films of Biograph, Vitagraph and other established companies with a regular turnover of productions? Producers were resistant to giving their players, and for that matter their directors, the status of a credit on the film's title cards, since this would undoubtedly encourage them to have false ideas of their importance. But whether they received individual screen mentions or not (and Charlie did not throughout his year's work for Keystone in 1914, either as player or director), the public and the journalists who were beginning to specialize in screen coverage for the trade press and the popular magazines, which were already reflecting the growing interest in movies and the people who made them, insisted on knowing who these fascinating personalities were. So the stars were named and, as the producers had feared, immediately began to press their employers for money commensurate with the attention they were attracting. Star snatching between rival producers became normal, along with firmer contracts for ever higher sums. By 1913, Sennett was paying his leading comedian, Ford Sterling, as much as

$250 a week, and Charlie at the age of twenty-four left the theater, where he was earning $75 (then £15 a week), in response to a final offer from Keystone of $150. Mary Pickford was to be earning as much as $2,000 a week from Adolph Zukor in 1914. Within a very few years both were to be earning millions of dollars as the two top-ranking stars of the international American film trade. Hundreds of prints of their films could be disposed of, and their faces and screen personalities were famous the world over.

Though both the stars and the producers rapidly grasped this new dimension in stardom, recognizing the unprecedented money it could command at the box office, they scarcely yet understood it in psychological or social terms. Irving, Ellen Terry, Sarah Bernhardt, or Eleanora Duse knew precisely what their relationship to their public was, as Sarah Siddons and David Garrick had known it a century before them. These great artists could test it directly in play after play performed in front of audience after audience, who acclaimed them and responded to every phase in the art of their performance. But this new kind of purely recorded performance, the film, had to be created in advance of exhibition, apart that is from the public, and the personalities appearing in the movies had to be chosen because the producers instinctively felt they could attract the medium's new patronage. At this stage the public for movies was predominantly working-class or lower middle-class, for whom film-going represented a very inexpensive form of regular entertainment in the developing comforts of the cinema as movie theaters. Lovers were finding the darkened halls attractive places of assignation; people who were tired or bored could sleep in comfort without offending either their neighbors or the players. The cinema was becoming a social institution which the public was increasingly incorporating into their lives. During the war years over four thousand "picture houses" were operating in Britain, while in the United States (with some four times the population) the number had reached twenty thousand by 1916.

The successful stars of silent film were voiceless images belonging, as has been so frequently pointed out, more to the world of daydream and wish fulfillment than to actuality. This was the new quality of stardom which failed initially to be rationalized. Great players of the theater were less likely to survive the test of audience appeal in this grass-roots medium than pretty young girls like Mary Pickford, who looked and behaved the way the majority of the girls in the audience wanted to look and behave themselves. Tom Mix, the cowboy star, and Douglas Fairbanks looked and behaved like every man in the audience hoped he looked and behaved in the eyes of the girl sitting beside him. The silent cinema provided a ready-made, standardized daydream to which the world responded on an altogether unprecedented scale. The familiar images of handsome heroes and pretty girls of film were supplemented by their portraits appearing weekly in fan magazines, adding the publicity of the cheap, popular press (soon to appear in lavishly tinted photogravure) to the glamour of the screen itself.

The stardom of Mary Pickford, Douglas Fairbanks, Tom Mix, W. S. Hart, and the others in the front rank was more immediately obvious than that of Charlie. They were "straight" performers. Charlie was a clown, dressed in grotesque tramp's clothing. But his successes and failures, his attempts at romance and love, his need for food and shelter, his desire to be accepted into the communities into which he wandered in need of asylum, were all familiar experiences that endeared this ever-hopeful, ever-resourceful little figure to everyone who came to know him on the screen — whether as Charlie, Charlot, or any of the other names he acquired in the languages of the world. He was the universal figure, the universal clown, the strange mixture of impudence and suffering which had given the clown his ageless place in society from primitive to modern times, at once the pet and the butt of mankind.

The clown has a long and to some extent mysterious origin in society, linking folklore with superstition, and the psychology of the human species with its secret fears and its primitive needs to assert some form of superiority. The insane fellow would become nothing except the butt of a primitive community were it not for the superstition that the simpleton, the adult with the "innocence" of the child, was nearer in spirit to the divine than ordinary, rational human beings. However, though clowns were wont to set the table on a roar, like the dead jester Yorick was said to have done in *Hamlet,* they were also beaten and treated like dogs by their masters. Kings kept jesters in their courts not only to make them laugh at those times they felt to be appropriate, but also to deliver the occasional home truth, like the all-licensed cartoonists of our times. The mysterious link between the King, representative of the health and welfare of his community, and the humble jester, who kept him in heart with telling quips, is epitomized in *King Lear,* in which the jester, the Fool, is at once simpleton and wise man; Lear's conscience, reminding him of royal fallibility, a creature he loves and on whose total loyalty and affection he finally comes to depend.

Jesters and clowns could take on many forms, and in the absence of kings declined into knavish entertainers exploiting people of lesser intelligence and sophistication, like Touchstone or Autolycus, who bring the unscrupulous wit of the town to bear on the comparative simplicity of the countryside. It was natural for such clowns, professional because they were good for little else, to be absorbed as characters into the written drama when the theater turned professional, adapting the "merry-Andrews" of earlier times into such clowns as Richard Tarleton or William Kempe played (often away from the stage as well as on it) in Elizabethan times. We have Hamlet's word for it that the clowns in the theater liked to improvise in order to steal the show for themselves from their more serious partners. In Italy, the celebrated commedia dell'arte originated during the sixteenth century at about the same time, or a little earlier, than the Elizabethan drama. It took the form of improvised performances following more or less accepted lines of action set down in scenarios, like outline treatments for silent films. The traditional players in Venice were called mountebanks (because they climbed on a stage) and charlatans (because they attracted a crowd). When at work, they were always to be found in St. Mark's Square. In the commedia dell'arte (the term implying, literally, the comedy of the professionals) appeared certain set characters, beginning with the clowns (called *zanni,* or zanies), comic servants who concocted all kinds of tricks in order to deceive their masters, the rich but stupid old men known as Pantaloons, characters with forebears in Roman comedy. Another knavish character emerged in Punchinello (Punch), with his hook nose and humpback. The romantic element was added in the form of the lovers, Harlequin and, finally, Columbine, while the militant, aggressive spirit in man was satirized in the figure of the braggart captain, who appears in Shakespeare in the character of Pistol, and to some extent even in Falstaff himself. Harlequin was something of a knavish figure, while Scaramouche was another version of the braggart, or cowardly bully. The commedia dell'arte was to become more influential in France than it was in Britain, where it nevertheless left its mark in the harlequinade, a comic piece played after the serious one in the eighteenth-century theaters (and later developing into the English pantomime), and also in the popular Punch and Judy shows, which linked the tradition of the commedia dell'arte to the far older puppet entertainments, with their slapstick burlesque and comic violence. The Italian puppet shows visited Britain; Pepys delighted in them.

In the harlequinades both the French and the English gradually came to sentimentalize Harlequin, making him simpler, more innocent, more graceful. He turned dancer, and was later to become the romantic Pierrot of the panto-mimes which the English theater first adopted early in the eighteenth century. The new kind of Pierrot was created by J. B. Dubois towards the end of the century.

It was Joseph Grimaldi, son of an eighteenth-century ballet master and pantomimist at Drury Lane theater, who brought the touch of genius to the knavish character of the clown at the close of the century, while the name Joey became synonymous with the kind of clown who was knave, mime, jester, juggler all in one, capable of every sleight of hand and body. His victim became a new type, known as the Auguste, dressed up in rags or finery in the last stage of decay, an excellent butt for every misadventure slapstick could pile upon him. He was later to be extracted from this secondary position by the great clowns, Dan Leno and Grock, whose clothes represented a burlesque gentility. These great clowns were all small men, like Charlie.

Grimaldi wore the painted face of the clown — a white complexion with red triangles on his cheeks, and a bald-pate wig with tufts or crests of hair. He was a zany of destruction and satire, though he was as much attacked as attacking. He was acrobat, juggler, dancer and singer. He was illegitimate by birth, and had had to endure his father's cruelty during his childhood, coupled with rigorous training in infancy for the stage. The voluminous notes he left about his life were finally to be edited for publication by Charles Dickens and appeared in 1838, a year after his death.

His performances were appreciated alike by Hazlitt, Coleridge, and Leigh Hunt. Hunt, for example, wrote of "his tricks and devices, his grins and shoulder-shakings, his pleasantries equally excellent, whether taken from nature or otherwise, his expression of childish glee in gigglings and squeaks, his facile dislocation of limbs carried about with an air as if he did not know it, his short and deep snatches of laughter like what we read in the poets about Robin Goodfellow, and his Ho! Ho! — in short, all these perfections of the clown which before his time perhaps were confined to the Italian stage . . . though he scarcely ever utters a syllable, [he] is a more entertaining and even elegant performer than many who talk well enough."

The very opposite of Grimaldi was the nineteenth-century French (although Bohemian-born) clown, Jean-Gaspard Debureau (Baptiste). Mime, acrobat, dancer, Debureau's special characteristic became pathos in the part of Pierrot, whom he played in the small, intimate theater of the Funambules in Paris, where he became the star attraction, though mainly for an audience of the working class, artists and intellectuals. In a sense he was the direct ancestor of Charlie, drawing on the cruelties and deprivations in his own life for his desperate form of comedy. He dressed in the loose, full, white costume with which Pierrot has ever since been associated, and adopted the melancholy, otherworldly air of the gentle, poetic clown. His pensive white face was that of the born loser in a world of harsh realities. He remained abnormally thin throughout his life, as if half starved. In fact, he never had money and was often near suicide. But he was a mime of genius, and no one who has seen Marcel Carné and Pierre Prévert's great film, *Les Enfants du Paradis* (made in Paris during the height of the German occupation of the 1940s), can forget Jean-Louis Barrault's delicate impersonation of Debureau.

Grimaldi died in 1837. Debureau died of asthma in 1846, aged only fifty. Following Grimaldi, high talent in clowning was not to reappear in England for another fifty years, when in 1889, the year of Charlie's birth, Dan Leno, clown of Victorian vaudeville, began his succession of appearances in pantomime at Drury Lane. Wearing his long boots, he had fantastic agility. Later in life he went mad. So the grand chain of burlesque, mime and clowning completes its link with Charlie, who was to become its greatest exponent in the twentieth century. He came later to recognize his instinctive link with the commedia dell'arte and the tradition of Pierrot, while of Dan Leno he says in his autobiography that he was "the greatest English comedian since the legendary Grimaldi," though when he saw him he felt he was "more character actor than comedian."

Behind Charlie's twentieth-century career, therefore, lay this long, complex and diverse tradition of clowning, much of it appealing on the popular level to the quick laugh at the obvious joke, the age-long latent instinct to mock physical oddity and mental abnormality, the cruelty of laughing at human beings in distress — though some at least of the uglier side of audience laughter was alleviated by their knowledge of the clown's magical properties, his resilience in the face of disaster, his quick revivals and comebacks, his spirited (though probably futile) retaliations. Clowns, like the type characters of traditional comedy, used comic exaggeration to burlesque age-old human pretensions, vanities, and vices. Sometimes, like the great jesters, they claimed the privilege of satire, knocking their audiences, and mocking public figures in their mime or gags. Mime, with its wealth of innuendo, was their most subtle stock in trade, while some allowed their humor to touch the fringe of sadness or, like Debureau, create a special poetry out of poverty, melancholy and despair.

The tradition in which Charlie was trained was that of the troupe, like the commedia dell'arte. Fred Karno's companies, formed at the turn of the century, represented the height of skill in the field of burlesque and the comic sketch,

all carefully rehearsed, timed, and executed, depending
alike on acrobatics, mime, speech and song. On the stage,
Charlie excelled as the comic drunk, the "swell" in evening
attire far gone in alcohol, requiring sleight of body and the
clown's traditional air of apparent indestructibility, skating
always on the edge of self-destruction. It was his success in
such comic mime on the American stage that brought him
the opportunity to enter the silent film, and he exploited
this kind of skill in his earlier films, most notably in *One
A.M.*, in which he plays the drunk solo for two reels, a brilliantly sustained piece of continuous mime.

But faced with an entirely new medium and an entirely
new kind of relationship between actor and audience,
Charlie instinctively put together a new character capable
of reaching audiences through an image all could recognize
on sight. He put together a new, twentieth-century Auguste,
a gentleman in tramp's clothing, a homeless man-about-
town, a penniless hobo of infinite social ambition, the outsider whose one desire is to be accepted and loved, the
perpetual outcast, though indestructible. One hardly believes in the few happy endings Charlie allows himself in
his earlier films. He is not above playing a rough trick or
two, like Grimaldi, but as the tramp character matured in
his hands he took on more and more of Pierrot's melancholy, and the spectrum of his humor widened and deep-
ened to include the ironies of man's fate in a difficult and
hostile world. The comic slapstick, with its occasional excesses of violence, a heritage from Keystone, correspondingly
disappeared. But happiness becomes more a matter of
dream, the lyrical compensations of passing illusion.

Charlie became the first true poet of the cinema, with his
humor a prevailing vein in his representation of life's sorrows. The mass audience, a mass mostly made up of needy
individuals, only too many subject to the hideous troubles
and personal losses of the First World War, of revolution

and a redistribution of power and authority, took the comedian, the tramp, and the poet to their hearts. His image was available in film after film at a cost of a few pence, cents, marks, francs, lire. . . . So, as we have seen, within five years he became the single most famous person in the world — a clown who posed no threat to anyone, and understood only the primal human need for love, shelter, and a few bright pennies to rub together. Millions of people out of work, or whose jobs might end with the week, understood this poet of poverty, of destitution, only too well and, consciously or unconsciously, came to depend on his recurrent adventures in adversity, and his ability to pit his small but agile frame against the demon Goliaths, the large-scale bullies and oppressors burlesqued so picturesquely by the "heavies" in his films.

Charlie has said in his autobiography, as well as elsewhere, that the moment this character was assembled — the comic, splayed-out boots, the stylish waddle, the ballooning pants, the fragile gentility of the formal jacket, collar and tie topped by the bowler hat of respectability, and the cane suggestive of city swagger — he took on a life of his own. Every comedian has had to have his "disguise": from the masks of the Greeks to the cap and bells of the jester; from the traditional garb of the characters in the commedia dell'arte to the exaggerated coverings of Grimaldi, Debureau, Leno, Grock, and the clowns and Augustes of the circus ring. Charlie at Keystone had to create his own burlesque costume, and he achieved it within weeks of his arrival at the studio. With occasional variations, including two appearances in "drag" as women, Charlie kept to this basic costume so that there was easy recognition even when (for example, as the drunken "swell" in *One A.M.,* the cop in *Easy Street,* or the janitor in *The Bank*) he had to adapt to the demands of different social classes, occupations or situations. He did not always appear as the simple tramp. The little mustache, further symbol of gentility and, with some twitching of the nose, of his fastidiousness, was common to all his male characterizations for virtually thirty years. Only in *Monsieur Verdoux* (1947) did he finally break away from it. There can be no doubt that Charlie had created a character with qualities of universality whom the public immediately recognized and adopted. The "little fella" is probably the most universally recognized comic character the world has ever known, this being due not only to Charlie's genius but also to the unprecedented scope of the new medium in which he was working.

The "little fella," it goes without saying, was a character conceived wholly for silence. Everything he did was created in mime, along with the infinite variety of his expression of face and body. As soon as Charlie had to voice him (as he finally had to do in 1940 for *The Great Dictator,* the song at the end of *Modern Times* barely counting), some part of his universality was lost, while the spoken narrations he added later to accompany the silent features greatly lessened the impact of the image, though they helped to keep the films themselves in distribution. These silent films are better left silent for people prepared to appreciate them for what they are, works of art from the era before sound, designed to be supported by music only.

When sound came to motion pictures in 1928–29, Charlie was only forty and at the height of his career. It was a staggering technical blow. *City Lights* (1931) and *Modern Times* (1936) were in effect silent films with recorded music, including only necessary dialogue for characters other than Charlie in *Modern Times.* But the question also arose whether the "little fella," voiced or unvoiced, was becoming archaic in the rapidly changing social climate of the 1930s.

The Wall Street crash reverberated around the capitalist world, creating depression, mass unemployment, and economic dislocations — which among other momentous things eased Hitler's path to power, the man whose mustache was similar to Charlie's, and whose youth had certain parallels of near poverty, self-imposed isolation, and frustrated artistry. The tramp figure continued to suit the mood of the economic depression, which Charlie in private life managed neatly to sidestep by keeping his capital fluid. Since the 1920s he had always endeavored to keep his reserves in the area of $3 million, in order to retain complete artistic control of his productions, since his feature films represented anything up to a million dollars investment each to produce in the studios he built, maintained, and staffed solely for this purpose.

But by the end of the 1930s and the coming of the Second World War, the "little fella" was ceasing to be relevant. The greater portion of the public was aware of more complex social issues than he represented, and aware of themselves as more complex people. The essentially simplified, symbolic comic figure could no longer embody, or universalize, the common feelings of the time. The "little fella" was archaic, and the medium he had adorned had overpassed him and become more sophisticated, more concerned with actuality and realism. Even Charlie admits he could not have made *The Great Dictator* (by far the most sophisticated film he had produced to date) if he had known the real nature of the Nazi regime, and had been able to foresee the mass genocide of the Jews and Slavs, to which the German occupation of Poland and invasion of Russia finally led. *The Great Dictator* was a film conceived when both Charlie and his public existed to some degree in a state of innocence.

Following the war, Charlie was to make his single dark satiric comedy, *Monsieur Verdoux,* and the "little fella" (still just present, though greatly modified in character, in *The Great Dictator*) had now entirely disappeared. The "little fella" only survived now through revivals of the older films, sometimes in horribly mangled forms in the 16 mm distribution libraries. Charlie was bitterly to resent these travesties of his work; he had no direct control over them, since his earlier productions were not legally his property until the completion of his contract with First National, and his entry into the partnership with Griffith and the Fairbankses (Douglas and Mary), which they called United Artists.

Consideration of the complications arising out of the total change of direction initiated by *Monsieur Verdoux,* complications for many valid reasons forced upon Charlie, forms an important part of the subject of this book. Charlie, when he finally abandoned the "little fella," had to find his feet with other characters and subjects requiring adjustment to new audiences in a more difficult, postwar age.

Charlie, like many other great artists who are individualistic, self-made men, is at once tough and vulnerable. Parallel with his astonishing public career, he has led a complex and difficult private life, which he would undoubtedly have preferred to keep private had he been allowed to do so. However, he does not mind it being known that he has enjoyed singular success with women; this his autobiography makes quite clear. One of his many biographers, Robert Payne, seems to regard him as a modern embodiment of Pan. Whether he is a contemporary Pan or not, his Pan-like charm, combined with dark good looks and compelling eyes, is more than a measure for most women, while his unique stardom and legendary wealth made him a target for ambitious girls right up to the day of his final, and fourth, marriage, to Oona O'Neill, which took place in the very midst of Joan Barry's paternity suit against him. In his unique position as the most eligible bachelor in Hollywood, it is only to be expected that his name would be at one time or another coupled with those of many women, some of them celebrated, others not. Even if he could have concealed many of these liaisons (or assumed liaisons) in decent privacy, the more gossip-ridden press was constantly on the watch to catch him out and start up some new rumor. More perhaps than any other star he has been the victim of his own phenomenal position in Hollywood society, and no biographer, including Charlie himself, has been able wholly to avoid discussing these rumors, scandals, and allegations, while at the same time deploring the manner in which he has been treated. It is a characteristic of the syndrome of stardom that it produces the disease of curiosity about the private lives of the famous. Certainly, his volatile love affairs are part of his nature, and many would class them as symptomatic of an obsessive weakness for women. He has been unusually susceptible to feminine influence, and his response to this susceptibility seems often to have been extraordinarily illjudged for a man in his position.

On his own admission, much of this need sprang from loneliness, from habits acquired during his wandering life as a youth, which took him on endless tours from city to city, where the heart is sickened by having to live in a succession of nondescript rooms in dingy provincial towns. Life in such circumstances can be transformed by a quick love affair, and the girls of the theater were no doubt equally lonely and welcomed the ardent attentions of this small, handsome and talented young Englishman with the cultured, musical voice. By the time stardom had been attained, the society of women had become a habit as the only real cure for loneliness — a new kind of loneliness now, born of wealth and the frequent necessity for isolation during the periods of nervous concentration which characterized the planning and preparation of the films. Charlie worked in effect without remission from 1914 to 1920, making during that period sixty-nine films, including many masterpieces of any length up to an hour (and in the case of *The Kid* an hour and a half) of silent-screen time. Like most

artists he found feminine company a great creative stimu-
lant, but his extreme susceptibility, especially to young and
mostly screen-struck girls, was what led him into trouble.
These were precisely the girls least capable of understanding
his varying moods and his absolute need, on very many
occasions, to be left strictly alone.

It is not the intention of this study to rake over these
difficulties at length yet again. They are only mentioned
when for some reason or another they throw necessary light
on Charlie's nature as a man and as a supreme artist of the
twentieth century. They contributed greatly to the grave
troubles he encountered during the 1940s and 1950s, which
turned political. They have been dealt with in detail in
books and elsewhere — responsibly, I think, by Theodore
Huff, picturesquely and overromantically by Garith von
Ulm, revealingly by Charlie himself, sympathetically by his
son, Charles Chaplin, Jr., and viciously by the American
press of the various periods involved. Certain of the ladies,
too, have given their own accounts of their relationships
with him, both troubled and untroubled, including Clare
Sheridan and Pola Negri.

There is no doubt that Charlie is in many respects (other
than as an artist-showman) a very private, inward-looking
man. He has therefore suffered acutely from the treatment
he has received, though he possibly does not blame himself
as he should for the naïve manner in which he entered on
his first two marriages, which could never have been anything but unsuccessful. The cost was to prove great in pain,
embarrassment, adverse publicity, and money. It was bad, as
well, for the two very young girls involved, though at least
they profited financially.

These marital disasters, coupled with the much publicized
details of his tempestuous relationship with Pola Negri,
could easily have wrecked Charlie's career during the 1920s,
when any grave scandals in Hollywood were looked upon

askance by certain powerful organizations of the day in American society. Nevertheless, he survived, his popularity in the end undimmed. During the 1930s his relationship with Paulette Goddard led to wild surmise, at least in the eyes of the journalists and the couple, even when finally married, chose to leave the matter open to prolonged speculation, perhaps just to enjoy leading the press by the nose. The publicity, in any case, kept Paulette Goddard's name in the news and indirectly fostered her career. A mature woman of striking good looks and marked common sense and sympathy, she, alone of Charlie's wives, was an established star in her own right. But this marriage, too, ended, and there followed the brief, disastrous relationship with Joan Barry and its most damaging consequences. Again, Charlie's career was in danger of being wrecked, and his very freedom theatened. With supreme, quiet courage Oona O'Neill, though aged only eighteen, married Charlie, aged fifty-four, and brought him in 1943 the peace, security and devotion he had needed throughout his life, and which he still enjoys.

By this time, however, political persecution had also developed to augment Charlie's suffering and finally to drive him forever from the United States to live in Switzerland. Once again, his stardom told against him; he was too prominent; everything he said and did in public was news. However, in spite of many hard lessons, he never seemed to learn to be discreet, or at least he did not manage to be discreet on every occasion. He chose for friends the people he liked, whether they were social conformists, such as Douglas Fairbanks and Mary Pickford, whose views were very established and right-wing, or individuals of the Left, including avowed Communists. It is ironic that Charlie, who in his personal habits, taste in clothes, manner of furnishing his house, and choice of elegant residence, represents the height of wealthy conservatism, should have become so identified with the Left, largely because he refused to say he was disinterested in the Soviet Union which, after all, he has never even visited.

The general suspicion, fed by the press, that he had left-wing sympathies came to a height during the war when, after the impassioned but wholly nonpolitical statement he inserted at the end of *The Great Dictator,* he was called upon to speak in support of launching the second front in Europe in order to help the beleaguered Russians, following Hitler's invasion and the United States' entry into the European war. By virtue of these speeches, which he made in various parts of the country and which reduced him to a state of nervous exhaustion, he became singled out for persecution when the time came for the postwar backkick against the political Left. After the negative reception given to the bitter attack he made in *Monsieur Verdoux* on contemporary society (an attack by no means limited to American society), Charlie was forced to live in virtual seclusion in Hollywood during the period of the investigations carried out by the successive Un-American Activities committees, which began in 1947 in Hollywood. Though at one time threatened with the possibility of a subpoena, he was never actually called upon to testify. He was always quite prepared to assure the authorities that he had never been a Communist; he had never belonged to any political party. But it was held against him that he had never taken out American citizenship; this was because he considered himself to be (as he so often repeated) a "citizen of the world." In 1952 he and Oona gave up their residence in the United States forever when a visa for reentry was refused him by the American Immigration Office. However in 1972 he was able to return and make his peace with the country where he had created his stardom and which, as he was at pains to point out in his film *A King in New York,* he still loved.

When as a newcomer he had first set foot in the United

States, he is said to have exclaimed out loud that this was the country he wanted to conquer. Five years later he had effected his conquest to a degree neither he nor anyone else could have foreseen, for they had not taken the full nature of the motion picture medium into account. His was to be a Cinderella story with slippers of celluloid. If Charlie can be held to be the archetypal male star in the history of the cinema — that is, a unique and entirely self-made personality — this is partly because the nature of stardom was to change with the coming of sound. As films turned mostly in the direction of ever-increasing realism, stars came ever more to resemble "normal" people, like the members of their audiences, even though they were strongly developed, as it were, the ordinary "writ large." Few, in any case, were to be great filmmakers, let alone poet filmmakers. Charlie throughout his career achieved everything in an art form in which multi-collaboration is normal. He produced, wrote, directed, composed for and starred in all his films, except only for the two in which he deliberately did not star, *A Woman of Paris* (a film which should surely be revived, in however restricted a form of release) and *A Countess from Hong Kong,* his last and least characteristic work.

The pattern of his life has in itself something of the structure of a work of art. Act One is his childhood and youth in London; the period of deprivation mixed with hope, of the great love he felt for his mother and the great sadness he experienced when her mind collapsed, of his hard but invigorating contact with the stage as child and adolescent. Act Two is his success in Fred Karno's troupes, which carries him to the United States and brings him to the attention of Mack Sennett and into the Keystone Studios. Act Three is his phenomenal success, bringing him wealth, fame and fortune, but denying him happiness and contentment in his personal life. Act Four is the climax of his grave misfortunes both personal and political, which finally drive him into exile away from the country and the people he in reality loves best, but who had failed to tolerate his human failings, which they magnified into crimes. Act Five brings the denouement of peace and happy domesticity in the paradise of exile by Lake Geneva. Such dramatic patterning is rare in real life, and helps add the patina of legend to the true story of Charlie Chaplin.

TWO

The Graven Image
of Destitution:
Childhood in London
1889-1900

IN THE SPRING of 1889 on April 16 Charlie Chaplin was born in the three-room apartment in East Lane, Walworth, a district in London situated east across the river beyond the districts of Lambeth and Kennington.* Shortly after his birth his parents, Hannah and Charles Chaplin, vaudeville artists and singers, moved to West Square, Lambeth, a small area not far from what is now the Imperial War Museum, but then the Bethlem Hospital. Hannah, a soubrette, singer and dancer of modest talent, who had appeared in Gilbert and Sullivan opera, and Charles, a well-established ballad singer with a melodious baritone voice, who was also not unknown on the European continent and even in New York, were both working and were reasonably prosperous. During her pregnancy and after the birth of her child,

---

* By a strange coincidence, Charlie was born within a week of Hitler. There is no record of Charlie's birth at Somerset House, and in the past his birthplace has been recorded as Fontainebleau, France — for example in the near-official annual Motion Picture Almanac until the year 1952, when it was changed to London. Others of note born that year included Jean Cocteau and Gladys Cooper, while the poet Browning died. It was also the year in which George Eastman produced Celluloid film, and Edison launched motion pictures in the individual viewer, the Kinetoscope.

Hannah provided vocal effects, singing echoing phrases to her husband's songs while standing in the wings.

Although Hannah Hill, or Lily Harley as she called herself on the stage, was only in her early twenties, she had had a difficult life. She was petite and pretty, with a sympathetic and charming personality; she was liked by everyone for her kindness and good nature. She was fair, with light-brown hair, and Charlie says she had violet-blue eyes. She is said to have been of part gypsy, part Irish origin, the daughter of an Irish cobbler settled in London; she and her sister Kate had run away from home and gone on the stage, where she had appeared with Charles Chaplin during his theater days. Then, according to Charlie, she had eloped with a middle-aged man to Africa, by whom she had had her eldest son, Sydney. She was only eighteen at the time.*

Charlie's father came of partly French, partly English ancestry, the French wing of the family being Protestant refugees from Catholic France who had settled in East Anglia. The name derived from *capeline,* a mailed hood. A member of the branch of the family remaining in France became an artist of modest distinction during the late nineteenth century, about the same time as Charles Chaplin achieved his modest distinction in the English theater and vaudeville. While Charles's brother, Spencer Chaplin, became a prosperous publican in Clapham, London, Charles himself gave up the theater in order to make his principal career in vaudeville, both composing and singing sentimental ballads. He fell in love with Hannah when she was only sixteen; they met when she appeared with him (ac-

* According to some biographers, Sydney was the son of Sydney Hawkes, a Jewish bookmaker, a first husband from whom she was later divorced. She later formed an alliance with Wheeler Dryden by whom she had two sons, Guy and Wheeler Jr. (born 1892) who remained with their father. Charlie does not name Wheeler Dryden in his autobiography. According to Garith von Ulm, the Chaplins had married in 1888, a year before Charlie's birth. Charlie himself, however, says he was born three years after the marriage, which would make it 1886.

cording to Charlie) in an Irish play called *Shamus O'Brien*. This must have been during the early 1880s. Charlie says she was eighteen when Sydney was born, and he makes no mention in his autobiography of her other relationship with the obscure figure, Wheeler Dryden, though their son, Charlie's half-brother, was later to work with him. Hannah merely told Charlie stories of her luxurious years on an estate in Africa, living "like a lord" with servants and horses.

As Charlie points out in his autobiography, drink was the bane of the vaudeville performers. The singers were supposed to drink after their act with the wealthier patrons in the theater bars, encouraging the trade in alcohol. Charles at his peak could earn up to £40 a week, and his wife, when working on her own, up to £25 — that is, some 200 and 125 dollars, respectively, in the currency of the period. On Sunday Charlie used to watch the more celebrated vaudevillians on their weekly pub-crawl down the Kennington Road traveling in pony and trap and decked out in checkered suits and gray bowler hats, their diamond rings and tiepins flashing in the morning sun. Kennington, like Lambeth and the rest of residential London, was thick with public houses, and they were by tradition associated with the vaudeville theaters and other places of light entertainment. Some taverns still had their music rooms, where performers could sing and dance and do sketches to entertain the customers.

Charles, a weak and sentimental man, worked hard but also gave way to drink, and this is what led to the final separation from his wife, though they had in the past been frequently separated by the divergent obligations of their careers. Charlie remembers himself as an infant playing on the floor of his mother's room and hearing her talk about her husband's failure to maintain her and the children, for Sydney had been incorporated into the family and given the

name Chaplin. Charlie has no infant recollection of his
father ever having lived in the same home, which changed
constantly, including rooms in the Westminster Bridge
Road, with its horse-drawn tram cars. Charles was later to
die of alcoholism at the early age of thirty-seven.

It was a depressed area of London in the 1890s: London
across the river, little more than a mile away from the
fashionable West End. It was largely a working-class area,
the districts of Lambeth and Kennington, reached by means
of the Westminster, Lambeth and Vauxhall bridges. Many
of the larger houses had already fallen on unhappy days,
declining into tenements, their tall and shabby facades
hiding the mean streets that lay behind, impoverishment
concealing outright poverty. The social gulf between wealth
and penury, plenty and brute starvation dominated London
society as it had always done. The population of inner
London had reached some four and a half million by the
1890s, and districts such as Kennington reflected the struggle
to keep ahead of the poverty line and stake out one's claim
to lower middle-class gentility. Girls and women without
resources quickly succumbed to prostitution or became the
prey of "sweated" domestic labor and dressmaking. Illiter-
acy was widespread in late Victorian London, though the
Education Act of 1870 had established the initial right of all
children to learn to read and write. Under the newly
established London County Council, the local authority
was only just beginning to face the vast task of improving
sanitation, lighting, housing and education. Primary education and social welfare had hitherto been largely in the
hands of charity and the churches.

There is a marked parallel to Dickens in Charlie's elo-
quent descriptions of the London of his childhood, Kennington in the 1890s. His mother was soon to fight a losing
battle against poverty. She was the stuff out of which a
certain gay and very feminine courage appears in the face

of adversity, but there were distinct limits to her strength of mind and body. She had two young children to keep largely by her own efforts, which meant that she had to work in vaudeville earning every penny she could so that Sydney could be paraded along the Kennington Road in a Sunday suit on Sundays, while Charlie was dressed in an infant's blue velvet with blue gloves. This was still the heyday of vaudeville; the famous original vaudeville theater, the Canterbury, stood on the Westminster Bridge Road, and there were over two hundred such theaters in London and the provinces at this time. The vaudeville theaters were not to succumb for almost another twenty years to the encroachments of that rival popular entertainment, the cinema; silent films were to become "items" in the vaudeville bills during the later 1890s, stealing their way into the popular shows they were later virtually to displace. Now, with "live" entertainment paramount, the artists worked hard, often appearing at carefully staggered times on the bills of a number of reasonably adjacent halls on the same night. The work required not only stamina but the ability to excite the crude susceptibilities of popular audiences alike with sentimentality and raffish humor.

With a child of five and an infant of one, Hannah set about rebuilding her career as a solo artist. At first she did reasonably well, but her voice, by nature weak, became increasingly subject to breaking and disappearing altogether through recurrent laryngitis. Her final appearance was at Aldershot at a place called The Canteen where the audience, largely made up of soldiers, were sadistic in their attack on any failure. Her voice failed completely. Charlie, who was with her, was hurriedly induced to go on in her place. He was five years old, and had already been taught by her to sing and to entertain family friends, singing such popular songs as "Jack Jones":

. . . since Jack Jones has come into a little bit of cash,
Well, 'e don't know where 'e are —

The audience, quick to catch on to a human touch, swung around in favor and flooded the stage with coins. When Hannah reappeared on stage with Charlie, who had also danced and done a few imitations for good measure, they received an ovation. But Hannah was never to appear in public again.

The little family drifted towards destitution, moving from the gentility of the three-room apartment to odd rooms in basements or garrets. Charles's ten shillings weekly allowance failed to appear. Hannah took to church-going to bolster her fading hopes, attending Christ Church in the Westminster Bridge Road. She managed to earn a few shillings a week dressmaking for women who went to the church, and she undertook odd jobs as a nurse. She pawned her jewelry, her theatrical wardrobe, and other belongings to keep the children alive. But however low her spirits, she always revived at the sight of Syd and Charlie, entertaining them with snatches of her old songs, dancing for them with the light and grace of her youth, acting scenes from plays. She was an expert mimic, and would imitate the passersby in the street, inventing stories and situations to match them. Charlie remembers that she once enacted the Passion of Christ, playing all the parts involved in turn. It was her instinctive way of passing her talent on to Charlie. She taught him observation of human behavior with the added quality of caricature. She taught him to dance, and Charlie, prompted by Sydney, earned a few pennies dancing outside public houses at the age of four to the tunes played by barrel organs in the street. But above all, Hannah insisted that her children maintain excellent diction; the boys' clothes might deteriorate to rags, but their speech must show that they were, in spite of everything, still gentlefolk.

Sydney was attending Board School, and sold newspapers after hours to add pence to the shillings which came in from his mother's needlework. After education became, as we have seen, a public service, school attendance was compulsory; education in elementary schools was entirely free in 1891, so Hannah was not involved in paying any fees. As winter approached, she made a greatcoat for Sydney from an old jacket of her own, with striped sleeves; she cut down the heels of her shoes to provide him with footwear. Her highly colored stage tights became stockings for Charlie. Sydney wept a little at having to wear his new coat; these strange guises got the boys into many street fights when they were mocked by other boys. Hannah's sight then collapsed through overstrain; only Sydney's lucky find of a well-filled purse on the seat of a bus while he was selling newspapers saved them. Charlie had his first sight of the sea as a result; they took a trip to Southend. He was never to forget the sunlight on the water, the gaiety of the colored lights, and the sailing ships skimming the waves.

It was in 1896 that Hannah was driven to go to Lambeth Borough Council for support. As a result, she had to face the final social degradation of being sent to the Lambeth workhouse with her children. Separation was forced upon them since they were housed in different sections. They were only allowed to meet in the workhouse visiting room, sitting together on hard benches, the boys with their shaven heads, Hannah in the dress of a Workhouse inmate. They sat holding hands and weeping. The stigma of destitution was too great to bear.

Three weeks later the boys were taken out of London to the Hanwell School for Orphans and Destitute Children. Charlie was seven and Sydney ten years old. Charlie was to stay at Hanwell for over a year; Sydney left in November 1896, when he was eleven, to join the training ship

Exmouth.* Charlie claims he was classed as an infant and tells how he had to submit to the indignity of being washed naked by the older schoolgirls, aged fourteen, on Saturday afternoons. At Hanwell he received his first formal instruction in reading and writing. He also witnessed, and on one terrible occasion received a flogging. The beatings, with the boys held down on a whipping block, were conducted before the whole school, the children requiring medical examination afterwards. These acts of official sadism seared Charlie's sensitivity. But his teacher, Miss E. M. Rogers, had recalled that he could amuse the class with his "antics and grimaces."

While Charlie was still seven, the family was reunited briefly in Kennington, living in a room at the back of Kennington Park. Charles was forced by the authorities to make contributions, to help his wife and family, but they were intermittent. Sydney returned from the *Exmouth*. But they were soon forced through reduced circumstances to go back into the workhouse. It was while Sydney and Charlie were attending Norwood School, to which they had been sent, that their mother had to be committed to Cane Hill lunatic asylum. Charlie says he was too young to understand, but sensed her illness was some form of escape. The court decided the boys must be put in the charge of their father.

Charles was living now with his thirty-year-old mistress, Louise, who had had a child by him, now four years old.

---

* There are discrepancies again over dates. Charlie in his autobiography gives few hard dates. He claims he was "a little over six years old" when he entered Hanwell, and refers to the fact that it was summer. It would seem, however, that he was in fact seven. The entries traced by R. J. Minney, a friend of the Chaplin family, in *Chaplin — the Immortal Tramp*, quotes (p. 9) the official entries of the two boys to the school: "Chaplin, Sydney John, aged eleven. Protestant; entered the school on the 18th June, 1896, left on November 18th, 1896, to join the training ship Exmouth. Chaplin, Charles, aged seven, Protestant. Admitted on the 18th June, 1896; left to return to his mother, 18th January, 1898." Charlie claims that he was at Hanwell "for almost a year"; the register entry gives him eighteen months at Hanwell.

Naturally enough, Louise was resentful at being forced to undertake this further responsibility, and made the boys help with the heavier housework during out-of-school hours, scrubbing floors, fetching coal. They attended Kennington Road School. Both Louise and Charles drank, and Charles in any case was seldom at home. Once, when Sydney was away playing football, Charlie was left without food throughout Saturday until the small hours of the night, wandering the streets of Kennington. He has described his first, unique experience of melody that night in a scene which might well occur in some film — a blind harmonium player and a clarinetist were rendering "The Honeysuckle and the Bee" outside a corner public house facing a square. For a brief moment, Charlie was possessed by what he called the "radiant virtuosity" of the harmony. It was over in a moment, but it was to leave a lasting musical experience in his memory. The magic was dispelled by the realities of the ill-lit streets. Louise came back drunk at midnight and refused to let him into the house. Charles when he learned of this was so angry that he knocked her unconscious by violently throwing a clothes brush at her head. But Louise took to locking Sydney and Charlie out when their father was away on tour, and finally the Society for the Prevention of Cruelty to Children intervened. Fortunately, Hannah was discharged from the asylum, and her little family was reunited once again in a single rented room behind Kennington Cross. They lived off Charles's ten shillings-a-week allowance, when it arrived, and Hannah's scanty earnings from needlework.

It was now, at the age of eight, that Charlie gained his first experience as a professional performer. He joined Jackson's troupe of Eight Lancashire Lads, half of whom were Jackson's own offspring (boys aged twelve to sixteen, and a girl of nine with cropped hair). Jackson was a man in his middle fifties, a former schoolmaster and a devout

Roman Catholic, qualities which seemed to guarantee his respectability in the eyes of Charlie's separated parents. He was married to a stern-looking second wife whom he had managed to make fertile in her later years. He took Charlie on, offering to provide his keep together with two shillings and sixpence a week. The troupe clog-danced, and preparations for this wore Charlie out. They worked in two or three vaudeville theaters a night, while in the provinces they also attended school. For the Christmas season 1897–98 they joined the production of the pantomime *Cinderella* at the London Hippodrome, playing cats and dogs. The French clown Marceline did a comic fishing act. Charlie as a cat did some "vulgar" business with the pantomime dog, to the joy of the audience and the consternation of the manager, who told Charlie if he did that again the censor would be after him and he would lose his theater license.

In the Lancashire Lad troupe Charlie aspired to have a solo act, and the admiring Mr. Jackson let him do one of his best imitations, that of Bransby Williams, the celebrated Dickens's reciter. It was not successful; Charlie's voice was too weak. However, his abortive aspirations included doing a tramp act and becoming an acrobat. He finally had to leave the company when he developed a temporary attack of asthma. But he had stayed long enough to perform in a benefit for his father, who was by now a sick and dying man. Charlie returned to live with his mother in the small garret which was her final, independent home, number 3 Pownall Terrace, a near-slum property off the Kennington Road. Charlie was to be ill for some months, presumably during 1899. Sydney was normally away from home; if not at sea, he was doing work such as hop-picking in the summer. Later in the year he became a telegraph boy at a wage of seven shillings a week.

There followed a lucky break in the lives of Charlie and his mother. They became the guests during the summer of the mistress of a wealthy colonel. This fine lady, an actress who had been one of Hannah's friends in the past, lived in a luxurious mansion in the fashionable area of Stockwell; she was looked after by four servants while awaiting the occasional visits of her good-natured lover. On the side, it appeared she kept a supplementary, dependent young man of her own. Charlie learned what it was like to live in style, though everyone had to disappear from sight whenever the Colonel arrived, usually unannounced. This applied especially to the lady's young man.

But in the winter they had to return to Pownall Terrace. Hannah was working now at dressmaking for a sweatshop, machining blouses at piece-work rates which brought her one shilling and sixpence (about thirty-seven cents of the period) for twelve hours' work. The maximum she ever managed to earn was six shillings and ninepence (about $1.70 of the period) in a single week. Sydney, who needed a suit for Sunday, could only have one at the cost of eighteen shillings ($4.50) if it were pawned each week and redeemed on Saturdays, which cost seven shillings ($1.75).

It was about this time that Charlie, aged ten, prompted by some instinct, glanced into the Three Stags in the Kennington Road and saw his father. He looked very ill, and his body was swollen with what proved to be dropsy. He was breathing with difficulty. But he beckoned his son in affectionately, asked after Hannah and Sydney, and then embraced him, kissing him for the first and only time in his life. Three weeks later he was taken to St. Thomas's Hospital, where he died shortly afterwards.* Hannah vis-

---

* Certain of Chaplin's biographers, for example Garith von Ulm, Cotes and Niklaus, and Minney, quote Chaplin himself as the source for the story that he stood with his mother outside the hospital on the night his father died, pathetically watching the window with its light. Ulm claims he was only three at the time, and acted out the tragedy for his brother Sydney in such a way as to make him "howl with grief mixed

ited him several times; Charles's youngest brother, a rich man from the Transvaal, happened to be in London, and paid for the funeral. Afterwards Hannah and Charlie returned to Pownall Terrace, where there was not a vestige of food.

Charlie, aged eleven, peddled flowers in public houses until his mother caught him and stopped him — "Drink killed your father, and money from such a source will only bring us bad luck," she said. He left school and took a succession of jobs — errand boy, boy help on an insurance doctor's premises, a page in a Lancaster Gate mansion, an assistant at a stationer's, W. H. Smith and Sons, and a printer's boy. The best jobs produced twelve shillings a week, or just over three dollars. Sydney became a bugler on the Donovan and Castle Line, sailing to Africa. Money was slightly less scarce, and Hannah's father even helped a little from time to time. Charlie picked up odd meals at such friends of his mother's as the McCarthys — Mrs. McCarthy had been on the stage. Then, one terrible evening, Charlie returned home and was told by the neighbors that his mother had gone insane again. She had long been suffering from malnutrition, and this had aggravated the weakness already prevalent in her mind. With the neighbors and their children looking on in awe, Charlie managed to coax her downstairs and persuade her to walk the mile to the infirmary, though she was staggering from weakness. Charlie was afraid people would think that she was drunk, but there seemed no other way; there was no money for a cab. She was received kindly at the hospital, but Charlie had to leave her. He went back to the empty garret in Pownall Street and wept.

---

with hysterical laughter." So legends are born, or cultivated. Whatever he may have said in the past, Charlie does not repeat this story in his autobiography.

Hannah was committed for the second time to Cane Hill asylum, some twenty miles away. Charlie, still of an age for compulsory school attendance, chose to avoid everyone, even the landlady who was sorry enough for him to give him a little food now and then, when he admitted to being hungry, and to let him sleep in the garret until she had found another tenant. With compulsory school attendance still in its infancy, appearance there could be avoided with comparative ease; Charlie did not want to be sent back to the prison house of Hanwell. He picked up odd scraps of food, and did casual work for an isolated team of wood-choppers engaged in trading firewood. Charlie was circum-spect enough to keep his foraging for work and food to out-of-school hours. Finally, after what seemed an endless interval, Sydney (who had been ill in South Africa) arrived back, bringing with him as part of his baggage a crate of green bananas. He also brought a small fortune of twenty pounds, in effect a hundred dollars. For Charlie, Sydney's reappearance was an ineffable relief. Together, in some trepidation, they visited Hannah, and were upset at finding her vague and listless. She recognized them, but with little sign of her usual excitement and affection.

Though, naturally enough, he could not realize it at the time, Charlie had lived through the most formative period in his life. Although he was still only a child aged twelve, he had passed through virtually every strong experience which was to illuminate his art. He had been born of "genteel" stock, as his mother had never ceased to remind him, and his subsequent experience of poverty, starvation, and destitution on the streets of Victorian London had been all the more humiliating through his knowledge, in the vague memories of infancy, of "better times." The years since had been measured in ha'pennies and pennies, and the relief which the smallest sum of money could bring to an empty stomach. He had known the place occupied by the pawnshop in his mother's life, and the anxiety of selling one's last possessions to keep oneself fed. He had known the harshness of landlords, the "flit" from apartments to "rooms," and from rooms to basement areas or to the attic garret of Pownall Terrace. He had had little schooling which counted for anything, though brief moments of triumph when his instinct for clowning had earned him the passing response of his classmates — when reciting, for instance, "Miss Priscilla's Cat" to all the classes in the school in turn. He had received the ha'pennies of passersby in the streets when he was performing to the barrel organ. And he had experienced the theater, first when at the age of five he had so successfully rescued his mother in her tragic humiliation at Aldershot, and later in the successful teamwork of the Lancashire Lads, and the work in the London pantomime.

These all formed part of a rich education to a child as responsive as Charlie. But there were other things as well — the experience of human nature in the streets of Kennington. Charlie was by instinct as well as by force of circumstances a "loner"; while most boys tore about the streets in quick-moving, impetuous gangs, observing almost nothing, Charlie was watchful, curious, even as the smallest child, about the way people behaved. His memoirs are full of characters he knew only as a child — for example, his old Irish grandfather, Charles Hill, riddled with gout; or Captain Hindrum, the retired Navy man who beat the boys at Hanwell with a dramatic flourish of cane or birch, announcing their names through a megaphone; Louise, for a brief while his foster mother, who lived with his father in spite of the violence of their quarrels; or such eccentrics as Mr. and Mrs. Jackson of the Lancashire Lads, or the ragged and derelict vaudevillian, Eva Lestock, whom his mother rescued from torment by streetboys, or Mr. Taylor, who made precision rulers, or the strange, half-secretive family team (including an epileptic) who chopped wood for a living and gave Charlie shelter and companionship when he was on the streets. But it was from his mother that he learned by far the most. Hannah and her two sons by different fathers were a close-knit, deeply affectionate family group, united alike in gaiety and sorrow, laughter and tears, although from the age of seven, Charlie had had to become used to Sydney's absence for increasing periods of time, especially when he was away at sea.

Charlie was finally to lose his intimate, loving contact with his mother around the age of twelve; she withdrew from the sorrows and deprivations of her life and remained behind the clouds of permanent insanity. But while she was still consciously with him, his life was lit by the sweetness — there is no other word for it — of her presence. She was, says Charlie, "small, dainty, and sensitive," and she had managed to put up a wonderful fight for the survival of herself and her children. After her voice failed, she had concentrated on needlework, working hour upon hour, until migraine forced her to give up. Although she insisted on gentility, good manners and good speech, the theater had taught her a thing or two about vituperation. "Who do you think you are? Lady Shit?" Charlie heard her shouting to a girl who had been rude, and who came back at her that such language was not suitable for a Christian. "Don't worry," said Hannah firmly, "it's in the Bible, my dear; Deuteronomy, 28th chapter, 37th verse, only there's another word for it. However, shit will suit you."

She was perhaps more a private than a public entertainer. Charlie remembers her performances for his benefit at home, imitating to perfection, as he felt, famous actors and actresses. For example, she mimicked (now and then with touches of caricature) Wilson Barrett in *The Sign of the Cross*. At one moment she would enact Napoleon, at another Nell Gwynn threatening to kill her baby by Charles

II unless he would "give this child a name." While she still had her trunkful of theatrical costumes, she would put them on and sing her old songs, such as the one about a lady judge:

> *I mean to teach the lawyers*
> *A thing or two,*
> *And show them just exactly*
> *What the girls can do. . . .*

She was Lily Harley once again, "the dainty and talented serio-comedienne, impersonator and dancer," and she had kept her playbills to prove it.

Inspired by her example and training, Charlie had learned to dance, to recite, to imitate and mimic, and to mime. Then, when she had done all she could, and indeed starved herself into a state of chronic weakness, her mind faltered and sought its own oblivion. Perhaps she knew that this real, living contact with Charlie was finished when she had looked at him with the pain of parting after he had taken her to the hospital. As they led her away she had looked anxiously back at him with a heartbreaking expression in her eyes he was never to forget. Although they were to live together again during the occasional periods she was permitted to leave Cane Hill, she lost forever her old spontaniety. She was to remain sad, wistful and withdrawn during her periods of lucidity.

Second only to his mother, Charlie loved Sydney. Sydney represented all that was left to him of security. For Charlie, aged twelve, Sydney at sixteen stood for youth and confidence. He was brisk and enterprising. When he returned, good fortune seemed to be assured. When he took Charlie under his wing, the sorrows of the nineteenth century seemed to fade. The graven image of destitution seemed no longer to be feared. They entered the new century together with the enthusiasm of youth. They had a single ambition in common — to make their way in the theater. This, after all, was their heritage.

THREE

Theater and Vaudeville
1901-1914

SYDNEY AND CHARLIE had twenty pounds and a crate of bananas with which to start afresh. Charlie says that the impulse to go on the stage was no sudden thing, and that he had determined all along to be an actor. The problem was his clothes. His name was down on the books of Blackmore's theatrical agency in Bedford Street, off the Strand, but he had nothing fit to wear if he were summoned.* One month after Sydney's return his luck changed. A postcard from the agency came asking him to call, and he had a new suit given him by Sydney in which to go. He was told that he could play the part of Billie the page boy in the play *Sherlock Holmes* on a tour lasting forty weeks, starting in the autumn. Meanwhile, there was another boy's part to play in a melodrama, *Jim, the Romance of a Cockney,* which was to be tried out in Kingston and Fulham. This

---

* It is on record that Charlie played a small part in a sketch, *Giddy Ostend,* at the London Hippodrome when, formerly a circus, it reopened as a theater on January 15, 1900. Huff is alone in maintaining that Chaplin toured the provinces playing a street waif in "an anglicized version of *From Rags to Riches,* a typical Alger story dramatized by Charles A. Taylor." No date is given, but it is implied that this came near the start of his theatrical career. Charlie mentions neither part in his autobiography.

was Sammy, a cheeky Cockney boy. The salary for both productions was to be an incredible two pounds, ten shillings a week! The actor H. A. Saintsbury was to be the star in both. Saintsbury gave him his part to read, and suddenly Charlie was filled with terror that they would ask him to recite it out loud on the spot. He realized that he could still scarcely read. But he was told to take it home to study. This he could do with the help of Sydney. The rehearsals taught him basic stage technique, which he had never learned and to which he took quite naturally. Everyone was delighted with his work. Charlie claimed to be fourteen, was actually twelve, and looked even younger.

The melodrama was not a success, but Charlie was described by one critic as "a bright and vigorous child actor," of whom "great things" should be heard "in the near future." He went with Saintsbury on the lengthy provincial tour with *Sherlock Holmes;* Sydney was not so fortunate, and had eventually to become realistic and take a job as bartender in the Coal Hole in the Strand. Charlie, shy of his poor spelling, seldom wrote home to Sydney, who was still at Pownall Terrace; Sydney, who wrote constantly, had to remind him he should correspond; they only had each other now. Charlie grew melancholy as he traveled from one drab town to another, staying alone in theatrical "digs." The other members of the company were too old for him, and he depended on the kindness of successive landladies to cook for him. He became, by his own account, silent, withdrawn and melancholy, barely able to talk to anyone. His only companion was a white rabbit, he says, which he smuggled into his bedroom and kept under the bed. He tells a horrifying story of Ebbw Vale, in Wales, where he stayed in a miner's cottage. Here he was shown one day a "human frog," a white-faced man with no legs, only toes protruding from his thighs. His father wanted Charlie's opinion whether he would succeed in a circus. Using his strong arms, the "human frog" could leap several feet into the air.

Then Sydney joined the company for a second tour of the successful play, during which Hannah was once again released and joined her sons on tour. Eventually another home was established in London, an apartment in Chester Street over a barber's shop. She wrote to the boys to say she had heard Louise had died in the Lambeth workhouse, and that her son, now an orphan aged ten, was being educated, in his turn, at Hanwell. Then the news came that their mother had suffered another mental relapse and had been sent back to Cane Hill; she had to be looked after for the rest of her life.

Charlie was to be identified with Billie the page boy for a matter of years in a succession of productions in the provinces, and finally in London at the Duke of York's Theatre, where Holmes was played by William Gillette, the original American interpreter of Holmes and the author of the play.* Charlie was now sixteen, and sufficiently recognized as a London West End actor to be given a place in Westminster Abbey at the funeral in 1905 of Sir Henry Irving, the greatest actor of nineteenth-century England. He also fell in silent, yearning calf-love with Marie Doro, Gillette's leading lady, who was later to star in American films —"Oh God, she was beautiful," he writes in his memoirs. When she went back to America after the run of *Sherlock Holmes,* Charlie went out and got drunk, a rare thing for him since he knew what drink had done for his father. For ten months he was to be out of work, and in the confusion of adolescence, he wasted his savings, as he has

* Charlie also played Billie in a one-act skit. *The Painful Predicament of Sherlock Holmes,* with Gillette and Irene Vanbrugh, which opened in October 1905 at the Duke of York's Theatre, and the part of a wolf in the first performance of Barrie's *Peter Pan* at the same theater on December 27, 1904. Charlie describes the former, but says nothing of the latter in his autobiography.

put it, on "whores, sluts," and occasional drinking bouts. . . .
"I was a worshipper of the foolhardy and the melodramatic,
a dreamer and a moper, raging at life and loving it." Life
was, he says, a labyrinth of distorting mirrors.

Sydney, aged twenty-one, was more realistic. He joined a
troupe of knockabout comedians run by Charlie Manon.
They, like other troupes of their kind, were comic panto-
mimists, performing acrobatic slapstick to romantic ballet
music, their movements beautifully timed. Sydney was a
talented performer, and he soon graduated to the leading
company in this field, that of Fred Karno, at three pounds
(fifteen dollars of the period) a week.

Karno, whose real name was Wescott, had been a plumb-
er's mate before entering vaudeville with two partners in
an acrobatic turn called the Karno trio. He was to become
a great impresario, founding a Fun Factory in Camberwell
where he trained and rehearsed his many troupes of performers mostly in wordless, slapstick sketches. He also produced burlesques with song and dance. He constructed his
own sets and props, and designed his own costumes at the
Fun Factory, and with a brilliant flair alike for publicity
and organization, he sent his troupes out around the vaudeville theaters in special buses emblazoned with his name.
His wordless sketches developed every tradition in pantomime, including the teams of clowns creating choreographed
mayhem with ladders, whitewash, custard pies, and the
like, or the pantomiming of drunkenness, trick cycling,
musical instruments which failed to play or fell apart, and
other developments of clowning. Karno prided himself on
the timing and teamwork of his clowns, and he insisted
always on quality. It took six months of hard work, he
reckoned, to build a proficient team who had learned exactly how to work together. Many famous English clowns
and acrobatic comedians developed their talents at the Fun

Factory, including such famous names in vaudeville as Fred Kitchen, Billy Bennett, Will Hay, Max Miller, Harry Weldon, Naughton and Gold, Sydney Howard, Stan Laurel, and the two Chaplins. His companies worked the halls not only in Britain but in America and the European continent. His name became synonymous with slapstick the world over, and his most famous sketches were *The Jail Birds, The Early Birds* and, above all, *The Mumming Birds.*

Charlie's adolescence proved a difficult period, as might be imagined, bridging his original career in the legitimate theater and his new career clowning in vaudeville, while at the same time including extravagant dreams of romance with such girls as Phoebe Taylor, the daughter of his land-lady of the period in the Kennington Road, a pretty girl of fifteen whom he found friendly but overvirtuous, and, a little later, of a dancing girl called Hetty Kelly, who was to be one of the main loves of his life. He was by now seven-teen, dark, strikingly good-looking, but often silent and morose, seeming older than his years. Conscious of his lack of education, he began to buy books and study. From the age of sixteen he was practicing regularly on both the violin and cello, playing left-handed.

He broke into vaudeville again through a troupe called Casey's Circus, burlesquing Dick Turpin and also a cele-brated figure of the time, Dr. Walford Bodie, a fashionable purveyor of patent medicines and a so-called "electrical wizard"; he made himself up to look like this dignified charlatan, and brought the house down by reducing him to absurdity. After this, he was out of work again for months. Syd finally persuaded Karno to see him, but Karno thought he was too young. Karno is quoted as saying:

Syd brought his kid brother along — a pale, puny, sullen-looking youngster. I must say that when I first saw him, I

thought he looked much too shy to do any good in the theatre, particularly in the knockabout comedies that were my
speciality.

But he recognized the brilliance of Charlie's miming and
his delicate dexterity, and gave him a special part opposite
Harry Weldon, one of his star comedians, in *The Football
Match,* a popular sketch in which Weldon played a goal-
keeper, and Charlie a burlesque villain trying to bribe him
to "throw" the match. His nerves strained at the lack of
rehearsals, Charlie improvised comic business which satisfied
Weldon and pleased the audience. Karno signed him for a
year at four pounds (twenty dollars) a week. Nevertheless,
Charlie was not popular with the company. As Karno put
it later:

> He wasn't very likeable. I've known him go whole weeks
> without saying a word to anyone in the company. Occasion-
> ally he would be quite chatty, but on the whole he was dour
> and unsociable. He lived like a monk, had a horror of drink,
> and put most of his salary in the bank as soon as he got it.

When on tour he quarreled with Weldon, who proved
temperamental if Charlie got the laughs. Charlie in turn
flatly accused him of jealousy. "I have more talent in my
arse than you have in your whole body," said Weldon.
"That's where your talent lies," said Charlie. He was not
likely to be popular.

Nevertheless, he was started on his true career, if somewhat moodily. He turned down the lead in a Karno sketch
called *Jimmy the Fearless,* an anticipation of the Walter
Mitty theme, the dream of an adolescent boy. Karno gave
the part, which most young comedians would have jumped
at, to another newcomer to the company, Arthur Stanley
Jefferson, later to become Stan Laurel. Charlie changed his
mind subsequently and took on the part when it became

free. Such sketches were to form the basis of his approach to gags and mime in films. He was constantly inventing, adding business of his own; Karno's insistence on quality of performance was identical with Charlie's own instinct for perfectionism. The comic situations in Karno's endless sketches offered a wonderful preparation for the future.

Syd and Charlie were earning good money now for the period, and they decided to set themselves up in somewhat more lavish accommodation. They took a four-room apartment in Glenshaw Mansions in the Brixton Road and furnished it, as Charlie put it later, like a combination of a Moorish cigarette shop and a French whorehouse. There was a Moorish screen, its fretwork lit from behind, and a large picture of a nude standing on a pedestal and looking down on an elderly artist about to brush a fly from her bottom. There were a couch and armchairs and a fine Turkish carpet, all bought second-hand. A cleaner came in twice a week. This was their haven — when they could stay in it. But on a typical Karno assignment they would be rehearsing in the daytime and at night they would be playing at the Streatham Empire, followed by the Canterbury Music Hall, followed by the Tivoli, dashing from one to the other in a Karno bus.

By nineteen Charlie, now a principal Karno clown, was seriously in love. Hetty Kelly was a Bert Coutts Yankee-Doodle girl who had eyed him from the stage while he stood in the wings wearing his guise for the drunk in *The Mumming Birds* — a long tail coat, a white tie and a flaming red nose. They spoke when she came off the stage, and by the end of the week he had persuaded her he was quite young under the aging makeup and that they should meet at Kennington Gate on Sunday. He arrived early for the assignation, and he has described the agony of waiting, watching each bus as it arrived, until finally she came. Charlie had drawn three pounds from the bank, and he dashed her off to the West End Trocadero restaurant in a taxi. He was in a daze of admiration for her youthful prettiness. The Trocadero was barely a success, since he had to show off and order an elaborate meal he was far too nervous to eat, while she would take nothing but a sandwich. But she let him walk her home all the way to Camberwell. They met again the following morning at seven o'clock, and he walked her to her rehearsal in Shaftesbury Avenue. Indeed, they met every morning. Hetty was only fifteen, and scarcely able to face his incessant talk about his adoration for her. She was frightened by his passionate, ecstatic obsession with her beauty. It is evident she felt unable to cope with such feeling. It alienated her, and made her behave coldly. When Charlie offered, in desperation, to part from her forever, to his chagrin she accepted this. Further attempts to see her proved useless. He had completely numbed her. The lost romance with the beautiful but unattainable Hetty Kelly was to become a recurrent motif in his life, though when he met her again two years later he found that he was, for the moment, out of love with her. This, too, was to become a recurrent motif.

In 1909, when he was twenty, he had his first taste of foreign travel. The Karno company played for a month at the Folies Bergère in the autumn. Paris enlarged Charlie's still-innocent vision of high society and worldly living, and he was so shocked at the charge for spending a short while with a superior courtesan with an expensive look to her that he felt obliged to abandon her on the journey to her apartment. Later, he was to visit brothels with other members of the Karno troupe, as he reveals in his memoirs. He had his first taste, too, of being received by the famous — Debussy (whose name he had not heard before) invited him to his box at the Folies, and complimented him — "You are an instinctive musician and dancer." Charlie was happy to be told this, but was actually more interested in the beautiful member of the Russian ballet whom Debussy had with him than he was in the composer himself. But Charlie had a right to be pleased with himself. He was top now of the Karno bill, and making a name for himself. Nevertheless, his voice let him down when the opportunity came to take Weldon's place in *The Football Match;* like his mother, he developed laryngitis and simply could not be heard. But his real talent did not depend on his voice. When his contract came up for renewal he managed to get a small raise to six pounds (thirty dollars) a week. Then, in 1910, came the opportunity to go to the United States.

The manager of the Karno American touring company was Alfred Reeves. His brother Billy had been star in the Karno sketches, including *The Mumming Birds* (called in America, *A Night in a London Music Hall*) in which he played the drunk in the theater box who interrupts the show, half falling over a ledge of the box and finally joining the cast on the stage, where, among other acts, he starts a wrestling match. The Karno company became a favorite recruiting ground for both the American vaudeville theater (which paid much higher salaries than Karno to star performers) and for the films, which were now fully established in production in several centers in America. When Billy was seized on by Ziegfeld to join the cast of his Follies, Alfred persuaded Karno to let young Chaplin take over the star roles. He had seen him in a skating sketch in Birmingham and was fascinated by his clowning, which he considered more original than his brother's. Stan Laurel also joined the company as Charlie's understudy. Sydney, however, had to remain behind, a star in his own right in the Karno English company. Charlie, now aged twenty-one, was given fifteen pounds a week (seventy-five dollars); Karno offered him this staggering sum in order to prevent him, too, falling into the clutches of the American impresarios.

The new sketch for America originated by Karno was

The Wow-Wows, a skit on initiation into a secret society. Karno decided to let Charlie star in this and the other sketches, which included *Skating, The Dandy Thieves, The Post Office,* and *Mr. Perkins, M.P.* The company sailed in September 1910, traveling to Quebec on a rat-ridden cattle boat and after this by train through Toronto to the States and New York. Charlie dispersed the rats in his cabin by throwing his shoes at them. Before he left, he did what he was to do so often when returning to his native London from America; he conducted a sentimental tour of the haunts which roused his more emotional memories — Leicester Square, Piccadilly, the West End. He had walked until two in the morning, and then sneaked away from the apartment at six o'clock without waking his brother. He could not bear to say goodbye, and merely left a short note on the table with his love.

The company arrived in New York on a Sunday morning. Times Square looked less than romantic, quite unlike Paris, Charlie's only other experience of being abroad. The remnants of newspapers were blowing about the pavements, spent and desolate. Men in shirt-sleeves were sitting about having their shoes shined. Charlie felt the tremors of fear experienced by a stranger alone in a new city. The tall buildings, the like of which he had never seen before, towered threateningly into the sky. Casting about for what he should do, he hired a back room in a brownstone house on 43rd Street. The old, familiar feeling of utter loneliness possessed him, but it was tempered now with the desolation of homesickness. Where was the familiar friendliness of London to be found among the aggressive-seeming automatons lounging along the sidewalks of New York? Only at night did the place begin to look human; the lights came on, and the throngs of people looked relaxed. Charlie, strolling in the heat, began to feel he belonged to the New World.

He appeared for the first time before an American audience on October 3, 1910, at the Colonial Theater in New York. He had to live up to the great Karno reputation in the opening sketch which he actually hated — *The Wow-Wows*. Karno had insisted it was just right for America, but with its modest, inhibited English jokes the show was a flop in New York, and Charlie felt crushed and humiliated by the silent, unlaughing audiences. In the highly competitive show stakes, Karno's name sunk temporarily through the weakness of *The Wow-Wows*. The company was competing with the quick patter of a diminutive Walter Winchell in *Gus Edwards's Schooldays,* which was on the same bill. Nevertheless, Charlie attracted a good notice in *Variety* — "There was at least one funny Englishman in the troupe and he will do for America. . . . His manner," wrote the reviewer, "is quiet and easy, and he goes about his work in a devil-may-care manner."

In the third week the company had a change of theater and a different kind of audience; to their surprise, they found the people out front roaring with laughter. It was a miracle explained, according to Charlie, by the fact that the audience in this Fifth Avenue theater was composed of English butlers and valets. The Karno stakes went up again, and the troupe, fifteen strong, was booked for a twenty-week tour out West on the Sullivan and Considine circuit — three shows a day. The tour took them round the Middle West. Charlie managed to save fifty dollars a week out of his seventy-five dollar earnings. Cheap hotels charged seven dollars a week, everything included. On Sundays, for ten cents you could shoot dice at the drugstores and saloons for the goods.

Everywhere he went, Charlie took his violin and his cello with him. America set him dreaming. The atmosphere was utterly different from London. Life here was a gamble with rich stakes. Poverty was everywhere; Charlie saw this during his endless, brooding wanderings, in the slums of New York, in the "smoke and steel" of the Chicago of 1910, in the sadness of the burlesque shows with their tired chorus girls and shabby sex. Charlie had his eye on the show girls, and stayed in the same cheap hotels as they did when he could. But behind all this seediness was a cocky quality that Charlie loved, the extravagance, the outlandish dreams of success which, what did you know, might sometimes come off. The show moved west — Charlie lists, among other cities, Cleveland, St. Louis, Minneapolis, Kansas City, Denver, and Butte, Montana, where the miners wore top boots, two-gallon hats and red neckerchiefs. Charlie records his fascination with the exotic red-light districts these towns boasted, such as the street in Butte with its handsome girls offering themselves at a dollar a visit. Then came Winnipeg and Vancouver (with English audiences), Tacoma, Seattle, Portland, and finally San Francisco (still recovering from the earthquake of 1906), Los Angeles, and Salt Lake City. He much preferred the spirit of San Francisco to that of Los Angeles, and he was taken with the extraordinarily wide streets of Salt Lake City. Back in New York City, the company was booked for another six-week season, which was successful. It was here that Mack Sennett, then a member of D. W. Griffith's team at Biograph, first saw Charlie perform. "If ever I become a big shot, there's a guy I'll sign up," Mack said, or says he said. The season in New York was followed by another twenty-week tour on the Sullivan and Considine circuit.

Robert Florey, who was later to work with Charlie, says that Alfred Reeves told him Charlie had the idea during this first visit to America that they should save up to buy a movie camera and spend their mornings filming the company performing their various sketches in the open air. The idea had to be abandoned when they went on tour. Reeves added that neither of them at this stage had any knowledge of even the most elementary film technique. Charlie also mentions these embryonic ambitions he had for filmmaking, and admits that he knew nothing at the time about what would be involved.

In the summer of 1912, Charlie returned to London and worked a fourteen-week season, including a visit to the Channel Islands, where he watched a newsreel cameraman at work and was momentarily filmed as part of the crowd. Back in England, he felt rootless. The apartment had been given up. His brother Sydney had married and was working hard. His mother's mind was far gone, and she was confined in a padded room. He was so horrified when he heard that she was receiving shock treatment with ice cold water that he arranged with Sydney for her to be put in a private mental hospital, where Dan Leno, the great clown, had been confined before his death. But England, in spite of his affection for it, seemed rather commonplace and over-familiar after the excitement of America. He hankered to get back.

He returned to the United States for Karno late in 1912, this time sailing on the liner *Olympic*. He felt much more assured — he knew people everywhere, and the tour which took him across the States to the West Coast meant a chance to see old friends, including a girl with whom he had spent a "romantic week" in St. Paul, Minnesota. He says that he lived alone, away from the rest of the company, and that he was intent by now on self-education, browsing around the second-hand book shops, discovering Ingersoll (and atheism), Emerson, Schopenhauer, Whitman, Poe, Twain, Hawthorne, Irving. The work nevertheless was very hard (three and sometimes four shows a day for seven days a week), and the minor towns, the "sticks," were drab and uninviting. In May he reached Philadelphia, where the company had a week "out," which at least spelled freedom. Charlie tells how he decided to go to New York for a few days and live it up. He stayed at the Astor in a room costing $4.50 a day. The sheer luxury of it (he says) made him want to cry. In America you were precisely the class you could afford to be; back in England he had still felt placed among the "lower classes" by the nature of his upbringing and lack of any recognized education. Yet the loneliness of camping out at the Astor depressed him. He went back to Philadelphia the following day. But he was not to forget his response to the luxury, the attention, the respect which was given him by servants, clerks, and the like.

Philadelphia was to be the place where he received the offer which represented the turning point in his life. The story has been told with many fanciful variations. Kessel and Bauman of New York, who Charlie thought at first were a firm of lawyers, wanted to contact a man named Caplin, Chaffin, or the like, who was a member of the company.* Reeves thought that this must be Charlie, and the upshot was that he took an early morning train to New York only to find that Kessel and Bauman were the owners of Mack Sennett's Keystone Comedy Film Company. He was disappointed; he thought he was going to be told he had been left a legacy by one of his remote and wealthy relatives.

Kessel offered him on Sennett's behalf $150 a week to appear in up to three films a week. This was twice his salary from Karno. He was to replace Ford Sterling, one of Sennett's principal actors, who was leaving Keystone to found his own production company. Charlie thought fast; he had seen Keystone knockabout comedies and thought them rough and lacking in finesse. On the other hand, a season in films at twice the money while free from the rigorous and depressing routine of touring was a great in-

---

* Charlie's version in the autobiography agrees with that told Florey by Bert Ennis, publicity director of Kessel and Bauman. Ennis was the sender of the telegram "towards the end of 1912."

ducement. He was also aware, he tells us, of the publicity value which films represented; they could make him an international star inside a year. So, having to make up his mind on the spot, he asked for $200 and left for Philadelphia to await developments. Sennett eventually agreed to sign a year's contract at $150 a week for the first three months and $175 for the remaining nine, the contract to start as soon as Charlie was free of his obligations to Karno.* This was in September. Charlie was willing to change his occupation. He had been clowning for Karno since he was seventeen, and now he had gone as far as he could go as a member of a troupe. He was twenty-four.

Meanwhile, the tour continued, and took him to Los Angeles. He met Sennett briefly after a successful appearance in *A Night at the Club* in which Charlie, made up to look much older, had once again performed the comic drunk. Sennett's powerful personality and "beetling brow" made him feel nervous. He lacked any sympathy, any sensitivity, or so Charlie thought. He wondered if he had done the right thing to entrust his future to this man.

Sennett was to have similar doubts. He tells in his memoirs (some of the sharpest and wittiest to have come from Hollywood, though often inaccurate) that he was a Canadian farm boy with little education — what little he possessed he had had to walk six or more miles to get in temperatures which went down to forty below zero in the winter. When he was seventeen, his family had emigrated to the United States, and it was then that he had for a while worked as a boilermaker. He wound up, as he puts it, many times a millionaire. He was born in 1880, and when he first met Charlie he was thirty-three. He was of Irish

* Sennett in his book, *King of Comedy,* claims Charlie's opening salary was only $125 a week. The dollar rate at the time was five to the pound. Charlie was therefore to earn the equivalent of thirty pounds a week (or, according to Sennett's account, twenty-five pounds) instead of the fifteen pounds ($75) he earned from Karno.

extraction — the family were, he says, "full-blooded, tough, and pious." His real name was Michael Sinnott. His artistic ambition had been to become an opera singer, and then an actor. When Calvin Coolidge was mayor of the small town where the family lived, he got young Sennett an introduction to Marie Dressler, then a comedy star of twenty-nine on tour. She helped him at the age of twenty to escape from his dollar-fifty-a-day job at the ironworks, and he began in burlesque as the hind legs of a horse. At least this was traditional. The hind legs were the part which did the comedy; the front legs were notorious for being "straight." He had qualified in burlesque at the Bowery Theater in New York and, like Charlie, had known the rigors of touring.

Sennett entered films in 1909 and worked initially as an extra for D. W. Griffith. He used his eyes and learned the essentials of silent film technique from the greatest master of the period. He claims that he was a strong walker and used to pace Griffith to and from the studios; Griffith preferred to walk rather than ride, while Sennett had to. Like Charlie and Mary Pickford (a rising young star at Biograph), Mack appreciated money. He was scripting scenarios; for example, he sold the story of *The Lonely Villa* to Griffith for $25. He went along with Griffith, Mary Pickford and others to Hollywood in 1910, and became a director at $65 a week, or so he claims. Griffith claims that he was only earning $50 at this stage, so Sennett's figure seems unlikely. Mack took to betting on horses, and so came in contact with some small-time bookmakers, Kessel and Bauman, who were interested to get themselves into movies. Out of this interest and Sennett's capacity for persuasion. Keystone was founded with a capital of only $2,500.

Keystone production had begun back in New York in the summer of 1911, but had moved to California in January 1912. Mabel Normand — with whom Sennett conducted a long-term, hit-and-miss love affair — and the comedians Ford Sterling and Fred Mace all left Biograph to work with Sennett. They had had no studio in New York, working primarily on location; their cameras, in these days of the patent wars, were strictly speaking bootlegged. Things moved so fast that Kessel and Bauman became devoted movie producers and distributors in no more time than it took to add up their profits, and the Keystone group took over a small studio in Edendale, east of Los Angeles, on their arrival in California. "We made a million dollars so fast my fingers ached from trying to count," declared Sennett, and he had the studio estate expanded to twenty-eight acres. Pictures were produced very rapidly; they were improvised, every likely occasion turned to advantage. The comedians poured out suddenly, infiltrating themselves into real events, with real police giving real chase, the camera perpetually turning. They made one hundred forty comedies during the first year. "We made funny pictures as fast as we could for money," says Sennett. "Our specialty was exasperated dignity and the discombobulation of Authority."

Sennett established a repertory company of people and animals — dogs, lions, chimpanzees, as well as new members of the team of comics, like Roscoe Arbuckle, the 285-pound fat man, and Hank Mann, the heavy, an East Side sign painter turned acrobat who was one of the original Keystone Cops, along with Slim Summerville and Edgar Kennedy, Chester Conklin and Ben Turpin, whose eyes were magnificently crossed. Sennett built himself a tower in the middle of the studio lot so that he could watch the productive antics of his growing team. He spent several thousand dollars on a huge marble bathtub which was hoisted to the top floor of the tower, and became his observation post. He did his best thinking, he maintained, in a hot tub.

According to Sennett, it was Hank Mann who first gave
him the name of "the little limey," Charlie Chaplin. He
had known him on the Sullivan-Considine circuit. Hank
was a twelve dollar-a-week bit comic at the time, along with
the rest getting into the nonstop crap game which went on
under the biggest studio stage. Sennett had to allow this
much license to the slaphappy extroverts who made his
films for him. There was no union to protect them; when
they were not tumbling and chasing they were working as
studio hands for their tight-fisted boss and the even tighter-
fisted Kessel and Bauman in New York.

Sennett has quoted the costs of his films when he was fully
established, and they are interesting. He claimed to spend
between $25,000 and $35,000 on each two-reel (half-hour)
film, but the studio broke even only when the picture took
$50,000 at the box office. Most took $75,000 to $85,000, thus
equalling in profit alone what it cost to produce them. Since
the studio did not produce less than one two-reeler a week,
and sometimes pushed the record up to two films a week
(not all films were two reels long) the profits were very great
indeed, anything between $25,000 and $30,000 a week. The
only people who were reasonably well paid at this stage
were the top cameramen, top directors, and the top stars,
such as Ford Sterling, who could earn up to $250 a week.
Carpenters earned $8 a day, but hired extras and bit players
as little as $12 a week. Rather later salaries were to rise
steeply — Ben Turpin of the permanently crossed eyes and
mane of wiry hair earned $3,000 a week in his heyday, and
was as close as Charlie with his money. Mabel Normand's
salary rose from $150 a week to $5,000, together with 25
percent of the profits in her films. The films themselves were
all scripted internally to suit the contract artists, and all the
subjects were original; the writers and gagmen were on the
staff, working under the scenario editor Vernon Smith, and
all ideas and story developments were supervised by Sennett

himself. Among the idea men was the youthful Frank
Capra, who soon graduated to direction. Between $2,000
and $3,000 might be spent on getting the story right once
the studio had developed its standards. Then the wild ones
got to work on it, such as Del Lord, ex-racing driver and
stunt man, who would do anything behind the back of the
Los Angeles police, such as soaping the road for skids and
then driving into the slithery mess at fifty miles an hour and
braking. Scenes were often shot at twice the normal speed.
The pride of all actors (and actresses) at Keystone was either
to wield with accuracy or to receive with unblenching cool
the large, "splurching" custard pie which covered the face
and poured down the person of anyone likely to be a little
too much on his or her dignity. Del Lord was the champion
pitcher.

This was the tough, wild and resourceful stable to which
Charlie had entrusted his second apprenticeship. It was a
gamble on both sides. Sennett had seen him once or twice
on the stage and liked his work, but he could scarcely
recollect the "little limey's" name when he decided to have
him traced and put under contract. Charlie was small,
nervous, temperamental, withdrawn and given to melancholy, but proud of his years of experience in making live
audiences laugh at his inventive mime. He could not avoid
feeling he might have sold his art for money as he said
goodbye to the Karno company in Kansas City and took the
train to Los Angeles. He had bought everyone champagne,
an unusual gesture for Charlie, who was not exactly noted
for his generosity. He preferred to keep spare money in the
bank.

Sennett first met Charlie face-to-face by chance, in a down-
town vaudeville theater the first evening he arrived. Now
that he saw him without his stage makeup he was shocked
to discover how young and slight he looked. All Sennett's
top actors were solid, middle-aged comics. It was still early

days for Sennett; he had just fired the unknown Harold Lloyd at the age of nineteen, and left the discovery of his unique talent to his greatest rival in the comedy business, Hal Roach, in 1914. Sennett was yet to learn how to develop the peculiar qualities of a Harry Langdon or a Buster Keaton, who were to join him later. If Sennett was to teach Charlie the techniques of moviemaking, Charlie (equally tough in spite of his initial nervousness) was to teach Sennett how to handle artists whose pace and concept of comedy were different from his own.

Sennett certainly did not rush him. He told him to hang around the studio and watch the wild men and girls at work. Charlie took the streetcar from his modest hotel to Edendale and was, he says, so agitated at the sight of the players rushing in their makeup across the road from the studio to the drugstore opposite to buy food and shouting in raucous voices that it was two days before he could pluck up the courage to go in. Sennett telephoned to ask where he was; why he hadn't shown up. When he arrived, Sennett welcomed him, took him around the studio and introduced him to the actors. The studio estate, or lot, looked like a converted farm, with bungalows, and barns used for dressing rooms for the men. Mabel Normand and the girls had a bungalow to themselves.

On the big studio stage, with its streamers of linen diffusing the sunlight which was still the prime source of illumination for the cameras, three films were in production side-by-side. Mabel Normand was in action for one film, while for another Ford Sterling (whom Charlie was replacing) was just completing a shot. Charlie claims that he had no idea films were made in this shot-by-shot, piecemeal fashion. Sennett underlined how everything was designed to lead up to the final chase. This only made Charlie feel more than ever out of place — he hated chases because, he says, they dissipated the personality, and the only thing of which

he was certain was that "nothing transcended personality."
He was struck, too, by the contrast between the roughness of
the men (a mixture of vaudevillians, clowns and prizefight-
ers) and the beauty of the girls, led by Mabel Normand,
Virginia Kirtley, Alice Davenport, and Minta Durfee,
Roscoe Arbuckle's wife. Sennett left him in the hands of
another relative newcomer, the comedian Chester Conklin,
who recalls having lunch with him on this first day:

> He was a serious little fellow, very curious, always listening
> and observing and saying practically nothing except to ask a
> few pointed and professional questions. He watched every-
> body all the time. . . . Chaplin was lonely and humble when
> he started.

For a few days he was left to his own devices, wandering
around the stages, his apprehensions raised or lowered according to whether Sennett smiled at him or not. But he
made friends with Ford Sterling, who took him out for
drinks.

In the various differing accounts of the tentative early
days of Charlie's initial adjustment to the rigors of filmmaking, Sennett provides one version in his memoirs, *King
of Comedy,* and Charlie another in his autobiography.*

---

* Charlie allowed publication in 1916 of a book called *Charlie Chaplin's Own Story* (Indianapolis, Bobbs Merrill). It was a strange mixture
of fact and fiction, and was eventually withdrawn. It was nevertheless
good, vivid journalism, as the generous extracts quoted in *Focus on
Chaplin* (edited by Donald W. McCaffrey; New Jersey: Prentice Hall,
1971) show. Although in its general tenor it gives the same story of
Charlie's tentative, nerve-racking entry into the work at Keystone as
the autobiography he was to publish some fifty years later, the actual
details are almost entirely different. In the early story, he watches in
terror as the actors go through their dangerous mayhem; he was put to
work at two o'clock on the day of his arrival at the studio by an un-
named director (not Sennett), working with a collection of rats which
were artificially colored in order to register photographically. He muffed
everything, and when Sennett intervened, he was put into another film
in which Sennett coached him patiently, again with no success. Finally
Charlie insisted on directing his own films in his own way, offering to

Sennett himself was the principal director, and after him Henry (Pathé) Lehrman, whom Sennett calls "a fake French-man." He had met him when working for Biograph in California; Lehrman always claimed he had been trained by the Pathés in France, but his origins were mysterious. However, he understood the technique of Sennett's primitive forms of comedy. In Sennett's absence on location, Lehrman put Charlie in a one-reeler, with the basic title of *Making a Living,* which was shot in three days, with Lehrman himself, Alice Davenport, Minta Durfee, and Chester Conklin. The situation involved rivalry between a newspaperman and an intruding go-getter, the Englishman played by Charlie; the plot was very slight and led up to the inevitable chase. From Charlie's point of view, the key scene was his interview with a newspaper editor with much comic business, including his posh cuff sliding loose down his cane and being neatly re-trieved. Charlie wore one of his English vaudeville disguises, a frock coat, a check waistcoat, a silk top hat, a bat-wing collar and a polka-dot tie. He also had a monocle and a droopy, handlebar mustache.

From the start, Charlie crossed with Lehrman, who was a difficult know-it-all with a hard line in comedy and who did not appreciate Charlie's attempts at inventive helpfulness

---

pay for the footage used at four cents the foot. He shot 2,000 feet of himself in his now familiar gear, and was an immediate success, alike with the studio and the public. He was to be always a spendthrift in using film, which Sennett, like most other directors, was not, though he edited his work down very tightly. The first Keystone titles Charlie mentions in this early attempt at autobiography are *Caught in the Rain, Laughing Gas* and *Dough and Dynamite;* there is nothing about the apprentice work, particularly with Sennett, which brought him his initial success. But the spirit of it all seems right, his nervous, concen-trated, obstinately ambitious desire to be successful, his anxious visits to the cinemas in Los Angeles when his films were shown, his watchful-ness of audience reaction to his new, more subtle style in clowning: "Then it comes — a chuckle, a deep hearty Ha! Ha! Ha! It spread over the crowd like a wave. . . . 'That's it! That's what I want! That's what I want!' I said."

over "business" and gags, and in fact ordered many of them to be cut from the finished film on the grounds that they held up the action. Used to the cooperative workout of business on the stage for Karno, Charlie reacted against Lehrman's crude, mechanical approach and open antagonism when he put up ideas which did not suit the Keystone tempo. As Sennett put it, "Chaplin was almost lost in the shuffle when Lehrman tried to put him through our fast paces. . . . He couldn't understand what was going on, why everything went so fast, and why scenes were shot out of chronology. He and Pathé Lehrman wound up in a major row, with Chaplin so embittered that I had to lay him off for a week to force him to follow instructions." In any case, Lehrman was leaving the studio shortly with Ford Sterling. According to Sennett the film, first released on February 2, 1914, was a flop. Nevertheless, Charlie was salvaged with a good notice in the *Moving Picture World*: "The clever player who takes the role of a sharper . . . is a comedian of the first water." The press, however, was confused over his name: he was referred to as Chapman, Chatlin, and even Edgar English in initial comments on his work during 1914.

Charlie realized from the start that his costume was wrong — it allowed the development of no real comic "personality." In his autobiography, he claims he first devised the guise in which he was to make his name throughout the world on casual orders from Sennett to "put on a comedy makeup" of any kind he liked. He hurried off and instinctively assembled odds and ends of clothes which created a richly comic contrast — baggy pants used by Fatty Arbuckle which swamped his slight figure in folds around his waist contrasted with an overtight jacket and a bowler hat which was also too small. The motif of oversize was taken up again by his boots, the vast shoes, size fourteen, normally used by Ford Sterling as the chief cop. The shoes he had to wear on the wrong feet in order to keep them on at all, and the splay-footed shuffle-walk he developed to go with his earth-bound feet came initially from memories of an old cabman in the Kennington Road whose odd gait, due to his painful feet, amused the kids in the street. For makeup he used the small mustache, cut down from one used by Mack Swain so that no nuance of expression would be lost, but also making him look older than his years. His obvious youth disappeared; no one bothered with how old the character was anymore. In fact, he became ageless. To all this Charlie added a little swagger cane, symbol of the man-about-town. He was at once tramp and city man, a hobo and a genteel man of the world. The whole guise was a study in contrasts which excited the comic imagination, and Sennett liked it at once.

According to Charlie himself, his first use of the guise and his first, tentative developments of a comic character to go with it were for Sennett's own film, a one-reeler with Mabel Normand called *Mabel's Strange Predicament*. His biographers, and Mack Sennett in his memoirs, have preferred to make this debut occur in *Kid Auto Races at Venice,* a five-minute (split-reel) film which Charlie does not mention in the autobiography, shot at a West Coast amusement park (some say in only forty-five minutes), in which Charlie drew on his past memory for gags, intruding as it were before the camera in order to steal the show from the kids in their autos. The memory, according to a story told by Alf Reeves to Florey, was of a fat man in the crowd at Jersey who hogged the newsreel cameraman's shots with officious gestures. Charlie told Reeves this was a natural piece of comic business if ever he made a film. So he drew on this for his own first appearance, the film being directed by Lehrman and shot in a single day. The film was released with another half-reel of "interest" material, *Olives and Their Oil,* only two days before *Mabel's Strange Predicament,* and could easily have been made just after it (or indeed in the middle of it), since films at this period were turned out so fast. *Making a Living* was released on February 2, 1914, and *Kid Auto Races at Venice* on February 7, while *Mabel's Strange Predicament* appeared on February 9.

Mabel Normand, according to Sennett, did not want at first to work with Charlie. "I don't like him so good now that I've seen him," she said to Mack, so Minta Durfee (Mrs. Arbuckle) was Charlie's first leading lady and was to appear with him in several Keystone films. But as soon as Mabel saw the possibilities of Charlie's new guise she changed her mind and was prepared to work with him; she was to feature in eleven of the thirty-five films in which he appeared for Keystone, most of them (though not quite all) as the tramp character in the first, more elementary phase in his development. Although Charlie gradually came to appreciate Sennett and be friendly with him, his natural instinct to confide in beautiful women drew him to Mabel Normand, who was not only a very talented comedienne, but a beautiful, responsive girl with a kindly outlook on life. She mothered him while he was at Keystone, and she later confided to Samuel Goldwyn, "They didn't really appreciate Charlie in those early days. I remember numerous times when people in the studio came up and asked me confidentially, 'Say, do you think he's so funny? In my mind he can't touch Ford Sterling.' They were just so used to slapstick that imaginative comedy couldn't penetrate." Charlie made her his confidante in discussions about work, about books, about life in general. As for the rest, as Mack Sennett puts it, "Charlie was considered an odd-ball by my team of professional slam-bangers," partly because he did not enjoy drinking or gambling, and was (or so they considered) close with his money.

This first year's work, spanning December 1913 to November 1914, was to make Charlie sufficiently in demand in the world's cinemas for him to be worth $1,250 a week to

Essanay when they took him on instead of the $250 which Sennett says he was finally paying him, though Charlie claims it remained at $175, plus $25 bonus for each film he made on his own, which worked out at about $200 a week. He achieved this by gradually convincing Sennett and the others at the studio that he had his own style in comic pantomime which, although slower than the standard Keystone tempo, was just as viable with audiences. He made four films with Harry Lehrman and one with George Nichols, another veteran director, and he quarreled with both of them. He even had the courage, or obstinacy, to differ with Mabel Normand when Sennett made her, at only twenty, a director over him. Charlie flatly refused to receive direction from her, though the matter was eventually settled amicably and they worked together as codirectors on five films, while Mack Sennett himself directed or supervised eight of the thirty-five films, most notably the feature with Marie Dressler, *Tillie's Punctured Romance*. Sennett found him "easy but unpredictable" to work with.

But what Charlie was fighting for from the start was absolute control of his own work, to star in films entirely of his own devising, and this Sennett finally allowed him to do, though only, according to Charlie himself, when Charlie challenged him by offering to put his savings (by then $1,500) at risk in the films for which he would take entire responsibility. Apparently, the final dispute over Mabel's direction came at the very time when the films featuring Charlie were building up demand in New York to over double the usual number of distribution prints. The first film in which he worked entirely on his own was *Caught in the Rain,* which was released on May 4, 1914.

During the early months of the year Charlie was absorbing basic film techniques in their simplest form: such as when an actor leaves the screen on the right he must reenter in the next shot on the left, or if he leaves the shot by walking towards the camera and thus out of frame, his reentrance should be into the shot back-to-camera. What was more a matter of intuition and fine judgment was camera placement in relation to each phase of the action — the choice of long-distance, medium-distance, or the varieties of closer shot. This was more than a matter of pleasing or natural composition; it was (he says) a matter of "cinematic inflection. . . . A close-up is a question of feeling." Sometimes a long shot is far more emphatic than a close shot. He instances a moment in a skating rink when the tramp, having gyrated all over the rink and caused the utmost havoc among the other skaters, recedes to a seat in the far background and surveys the scene of his triumphs, a minute figure with all the damage laid out in the foreground. A close-up would have ruined the comic effect. Charlie had to learn how to break up the comic action he improvised into a series of shots which cumulatively built up and emphasized whatever was being done. This required real experience, and this is what he acquired at Keystone; he felt, as he said: "on the threshold of something wonderful," while his development of movement and pantomime taught the Keystone comics a great deal. He enjoyed the freedom to improvise from scratch which each new film provided, work which seemed fresh and exciting following the night-after-night repetition performing the same sketches in the theater. Sometimes the films were made at incredible speed; Charlie claims the one-reeler *Twenty Minutes of Love* was shot in a single afternoon. *Dough and Dynamite,* a two-reeler, took nine days and went over Sennett's $1,000 immediate budget limit to $1,800.* A week was the normal time allowed for a two-reeler. But *Dough and Dynamite* (released October 26,

---

* The figure given by Sennett above for the cost of a two-reeler, $25,000 and more, obviously involved total studio overhead, salaries and the like. The costs referred to here must be incidental, excluding such overhead.

1914) was, according to Sennett, the film which finally clinched Charlie as a great comedian with the public.

Charlie therefore built up his initial reputation with the public without introducing any of the sympathy or pathos which he was to develop in later films. The tramp at this stage was a real vagabond, a compound (admits Sennett) of cruelty, venality, treachery, larceny and lechery. The point is that Charlie carried out his nefarious business with such charm, gaiety and adroitness, while looking either innocent or pathetic, that the world responded happily to such an engaging villain. Nor did the tramp character always appear in the same clothes, though Charlie kept to the same overall appearance of disintegrating gentility. But the coats, waistcoats, trousers varied, and in several films he had to adopt occupational-style clothes, as in *Dough and Dynamite* or *Caught in a Cabaret,* while in *His Prehistoric Past* he was dressed in a skin and a bowler hat. In *Cruel, Cruel Love* he portrays a rich man, while in *Mabel at the Wheel* he owns a motorcar and wears a long frock coat and a tall hat. In some he appeared without his familiar makeup — in *Tango Tangles,* and at the beginning of *The Masquerade.* In *A Busy Day* he plays a virago wife.

The gags in a Keystone film usually arose out of some selected place or environment or occupation (the hotel lobby, a ballroom, a boarding house, a cabaret, the hotel bedroom, a dentist's office, or the combined bakery and restaurant of *Dough and Dynamite*), and ended in some kind of violent climax, involving a chase. Sennett claims that he accepted in Charlie's case that the trademark action of a Keystone film — the chase sequence and the throwing of pies — would not necessarily appear. Charlie's gags, he says, were furtive and subtle, and such violent climaxes rarely suited him. Nevertheless, there is plenty of slapstick in these early films, and chases do occur. Charlie developed his celebrated corner-turning act while on the run — hopping as he turned as if applying brakes before dashing on out of sight of his pursuers.

In *Mabel's Strange Predicament,* the first full-length comedy ever made, Charlie, an intrusive tramp, creates havoc in a hotel lobby, and pursues Mabel in and out of rooms; in *Tango Tangles,* he and Ford Sterling, neither wearing makeup, cause trouble chasing a hat-check girl in a real ballroom; several films, such as *The Star Boarder, Mabel at the Wheel, Twenty Minutes of Love, Caught in the Rain, His Trysting Place* and *Getting Acquainted* are all dependent on jealousy, rivalry, infidelity in love and marriage, while in a number of the Keystone films Charlie is drunk in the style of a Karno sketch, for example in *The Rounders,* with Fatty Arbuckle, and in *His Favorite Pastime.* Violence of some kind is common to most of the films, involving kicking, pin-sticking, coshing with any weapons to hand (Mabel hits unfaithful Charlie with an ironing board in *His Trysting Place*), and spectacular falls — in *His Favorite Pastime,* Charlie turns a somersault over a staircase banister and lands rightway up on a sofa, still smoking a cigarette. The Keystone obsession with pie or flour-bag throwing occurs only in *Caught in a Cabaret* and *Dough and Dynamite.* In *A Film Johnnie,* Charlie manages to ruin several scenes being shot at Keystone. There are many brilliantly acted little gags in these films — having absorbed water from a hose, Charlie gives his ear a twist and spouts a jet of water out of his mouth (in *A Film Johnnie*); jealous of a couple making love in a park, Charlie puts his arms around a tree (in *Twenty Minutes of Love*); crossing his legs when posing as a duke in *Caught in a Cabaret,* Charlie the waiter, while flirting with Mabel, suddenly reveals a hole in the sole of his shoe and immediately hangs his hat on his toe. Charlie produces doughnuts by twisting hanks of dough around his wrists like bracelets in *Dough and Dynamite,* and as the new overlord in *His Prehistoric Past,* struts majestically over the prone bodies of the girls in his cave-man entourage. In *The Rounders* he suddenly strikes a match on an irate man's bald head, and in *The New Janitor* performs the famous trick of leaning over, picking up a pistol, covering a crook with it between his legs, and then straightening up by stepping over his hands while still covering the thief.

It is wrong to dismiss these films as five-finger exercises because of their obvious simplicity of situation and the crudity of much of the action. Seen today, the utter ruthless-ness of the fun detracts at times from the exuberance of the film as a whole — sticking a pin in Mabel's thigh in *Dough and Dynamite* overspills. The violence is only offset by the resilience of recovery in the Keystone clowns, but the slightest suggestion of real as opposed to "playful pain" destroys the farcical illusion.

The feature *Tillie's Punctured Romance* was based on a musical comedy, *Tillie's Nightmare,* in which Marie Dressler plays the vast country girl whom Charlie's slightly built "city slicker" betrays, stealing her money and going off with his real girl, Mabel. When Tillie inherits three million dollars, Charlie returns to the pursuit and marries her, and there is much comic jealousy — Tillie firing off pistols, and the Keystone Kops joining in the final chase. There is a delightful burlesque tango danced by Tillie and Charlie, but the film, though deriving some strength from a good story, gave Charlie comparatively little opportunity to show his real worth, considering it is of feature length. The excessive resort to mere kicking is tedious and tasteless.

Both Charlie and Mack were hard men when it came to money. They were looking at each other askance toward the end of 1914; Charlie's contract was due to run out in mid-December. Charlie, thinking his luck might expire, claims his demand to Sennett was for $1,000 a week. Rather than take less, Charlie felt it might pay him to produce his own movies. Eventually, Essanay (George K. Spoor and "Bronco Billy" Anderson, S and A) came up with an offer of $1,250 a week and (according to their representatives) a bonus on signing of $10,000. Charlie accepted, but had to go to Chicago to sign. Finishing cutting *His Prehistoric Past* on a Saturday, he went off to Chicago the following Monday along with Anderson, who proved somewhat reticent about the bonus. When they reached Chicago, Spoor was away until New Year's Day, and there was still no money. Anderson left for his studio at Niles, near San Francisco, where he made Westerns, and Charlie, increasingly annoyed at the nonarrival of Spoor, started work on his first film for Essanay, called *His New Job,* a satiric burlesque on the making of a film star still conceived in the Keystone style. He worked with players on the Essanay payroll, Charlotte Mineau, Leo White, and the cross-eyed comedian, Ben Turpin. The studio was called Lockstone.

Spoor had in fact fled from Chicago because he thought his partner had gone mad when he had heard of the terms of the deal with Charlie, a comedian of whom it would appear he had never heard. When he eventually returned in the middle of January, he tested Charlie's reputation in a hotel lobby in Chicago by having him paged. The rush to see Charlie was sufficient to prove he had a success on his hands. He had in fact secured a bargain. News of Charlie's new film had also leaked out, and the bidding for prints was high. So Charlie got his money, accompanied by profuse apologies, and, having finished *His New Job,* a two-reeler, he asked to be moved from wintry Chicago to Niles, since he preferred working in the warmth of California.

Here the second phase of his career in films began, and was to achieve a response from the public far beyond his dreams at Keystone.

❦

FOUR

Fame with Art
1915-1936

CHARLIE WAS TO MAKE FIVE FILMS at Bronco Billy's bare and ill-equipped studios at Niles, an isolated rural community an hour's drive from San Francisco; from April 1915 the rest of his total Essanay assignment of fourteen films were made in hired studios at Los Angeles, after he had found the studio at Niles impossible to work in, since it was really only suitable for Bronco Billy's Westerns. Although a multimillionaire, Bronco Billy was an "eccentric," satisfied with the barest essentials both in his studio and the Spartan bungalow in which he lived when working at Niles. Charlie, with his hankering after luxury, was horrified.

Charlie found at Essanay a responsive cameraman, Rollie Totheroh, who was to stay with him throughout his career in the States. He was a young man, a year younger than Charlie, and he had a difficult assignment this first year, using artificial light in Chicago, sunlight assisted now and then with artificial light at Niles, and varied conditions in the hired studios in Los Angeles — first at the Bradbury Studio in North Hill Street and later in the larger but antiquated Majestic Studio on Fairview Avenue. Regular Essanay actors, notably Leo White, Ben Turpin, Lloyd

Bacon, Bud Jamieson, Billy Armstrong, John Rand and Paddy McGuire, formed the main stock company for the films, along with Wesley Ruggles, who was later to become a well-known Hollywood director. Leo White was a stage artist from musical comedy, Bud Jamieson a nonprofessional chosen for his huge size, Billy Armstrong a former Karno clown, while John Rand came from the circus.

Charlie was also to acquire a leading lady who was to stay with him longer than any other and feature in no fewer than thirty-five of his films, from *A Night Out* (February 1915) to *A Woman of Paris* (1923) — all in fact except his own solo film, *One A.M.*, made the following year for Mutual. This was Edna Purviance, a college girl from Lovelock, Nevada, with no acting experience. She appealed to Charlie the moment he was introduced to her because of her beauty, her reserve, and her sad expression. She was twenty and, apparently, was just getting over a broken love affair. Charlie took a chance on her; at least she would be decorative, and like Mack Sennett he knew that beautiful girls had an important part to play in burlesque because of the strong undercurrent of sex on which it thrived.

Charlie was now, in effect, an independent creator. As long as he delivered the films his employers did not interfere with what he chose to do. Indeed, there were no rivals in his field, as there had been at Keystone, and no critical expert, like Mack Sennett, to breathe down his neck and insist on the Keystone hallmark in the nature of his work. Producing a film at approximately three-weekly intervals, instead of weekly, Charlie had more leisure to invent and improvise on the studio floor, and his fourteen films for Essanay contained a far higher proportion of two-reelers (playing up to half an hour), including a burlesque on the *Carmen* story as it had been filmed recently by Cecil B. De Mille, and also by Fox with Theda Bara. Essanay very improperly expanded *Carmen* from its original two to four reels after Charlie's departure to Mutual, padding it out by adding a new subplot featuring Ben Turpin. Charlie was to sue them on its release the following year.*

Charlie still preferred to work without a developed script, improvising the action on the studio floor inspired by the set and the props. He prepared an advance outline only to give the film a firm structure. He capitalized on his work for Keystone, and gave his films greater weight, turning burlesque in the direction of satire. Even in his first film, *His New Job* (February 1915), he mocked the contemporary inflated romantic movie dramas in his burlesque handling of Charlie the star-hero swamped in a vast shako and an absurdly Ruritanian uniform, trampling on his leading lady's skirt and ripping it off, or performing a beautiful balancing act on the set with a swaying studio column. Not all the films he made in this highly productive year were equal to his best — with less than a year's experience behind him as a director he could not succeed every time — but when in doubt he could always fall back on the Keystone style of gag. In *A Night Out* (February 1915) he and Ben Turpin elaborated for two reels on the inability of a pair of drunks to cope with their surroundings — first a restaurant and then a hotel. As Theodore Huff has pointed out, *In the Park* (March 1915), with Charlie as the flirtatious tramp in conflict with a cop, is a remake of *Twenty Minutes of Love*. *The Jitney Elopement* (April 1915) makes the most of a Ford car (a contemporary butt for fun) — Charlie at one

---

* Essanay behaved badly after Charlie had left them. In addition to padding out *Carmen,* they reedited another of Charlie's films, *Police* (March 1916), and created as late as 1918 a bogus new Chaplin film, *Triple Trouble,* assembled out of bits and pieces from *Police, Work,* and other genuine films, supplemented by new, non-Chaplin material. They also issued *The Essanay-Chaplin Revue of 1916,* a five-reel anthology made from some of his Essanay pictures, while in 1918 *Chase Me, Charlie* appeared in Britain, a seven-reel anthology of Charlie's Essanay work. This proved to Charlie he must safeguard himself against subsequent interference with his work, by insisting on appropriate clauses in his future contracts.

point starts it with a coin in the slot and a chase following an elopement. *A Night in the Show* (November 1915) goes back to Karno, using gags similar to those of the drunk in *A Night in an English Music-Hall*. *Work* (June 1915) also goes back to Karno and vaudeville in the mayhem of papering and decorating a room, though it has an almost surrealist opening (anticipating Beckett and the relationship of Pozzo and Lucky in *Waiting for Godot*); Charlie is harnessed to an overloaded truck and driven up a steep hill by his bullying employer, the decorator, who wields a whip. The camera is set low and looks up to the diminutive figure struggling with his load on the skyline of the steep slope. But the gags are normally violent, with continual use of the decorator's plank swung around to hit now one, now another man on the head; water is spouted at people through Charlie's mouth, or they are knocked down and casually walked over. Charlie makes neat use of a nude statuette to suggest the tramp paperhanger's shy but obsessive interest in sex; using skillful pantomime, he tells Edna the sad story of his life. *Shanghaied* (October 1915) is largely a roughhouse with heads being knocked with a mallet, and neatly timed action as the characters interchange food on plates sliding in a violently rocking ship at sea. *A Woman* (July 1915) sees Charlie in the burlesque performance of a coy lady with whom all the men try to flirt, while he has constant difficulties with his "falsies," improvised from pincushions. Charlie works the coy aspect of contemporary sex in the manner in which he divests a "female" dummy of its clothes. The short one-reeler *By the Sea* (April 1915) clearly improvised quickly on a beach, exploits the excellent gag of a high wind blowing off hats attached to their owners by long strings, with hats and owners getting hopelessly irate and tangled. All these films, basically knockabout comedy, have their brilliant moments, and most will keep an audience of any age or period in continuous, infectious laughter, inspired more by the skill and perfect timing of the action than by the originality or invention in the gags themselves.

The Champion (March 1915) is another case in point. The situation is of the simplest, and linked to that in the Keystone film, *The Knockout*. Charlie, down and out, tricks his way into a job as sparring partner in a rough-and-tumble boxing booth. His slight frame makes him utterly unsuitable to stand up to the beetle-browed heavies in the ring, but a horseshoe in his oversize boxing glove has helped him achieve an initial victory. He also has his faithful bulldog with him, which refuses his half of Charlie's last frankfurter until it has been salted for him. Charlie indulges in sleight of hand with the props for training — Indian clubs, weights and so forth. The fight with the massive Bud Jamieson becomes a brilliant pantomime of feints, avoidances, and whirling fists, a balletic burlesque of fisticuffs, falls, miraculous recoveries, and ploys with the highly elastic ropes which surround the ring. Finally the bulldog, hanging onto the seat of Bud's pants, gives Charlie the opportunity to lam his way to victory. The film is an extraordinary example of how the crudest, most elementary humor can be lifted to levels of delicate, finely timed pantomime, with the added subtleties derived from Charlie's fond relationship with his dog.

But in the evolution of the so-called tramp character, the two films which mark the sure step forward are *The Bank* (August 1915) and *The Tramp* (April 1915). The screen Charlie had been for a full year, both at Essanay and Keystone, an eclectic figure of misfortune. He had gradually moved away from the burlesque villain who gets into countless scrapes and emerges from them with engaging ingenuity to the far more appealing "down-and-out," hanging onto odd jobs by the skin of his teeth, more victim than victor in most situations, an impertinent David thumbing his nose at a variety of burlesque Goliaths. Looking back over the films, although Charlie's now-famous costume was in almost all instances an ill-fitting assembly of other people's clothes which seemed to reflect his desire to represent himself as some kind of "gentleman" fallen on evil days, the character himself was a comic chameleon who could become anything the situation demanded — not only a waiter, an ex-convict or petty crook, a prop man in a vaudeville theater, a janitor, a cook, a baker's, a piano-mover's or a paperhanger's assistant, but also an errant husband, a city slicker, a film actor, and a fake boxer. In one film he was even a man of wealth trying ineffectually to commit suicide for love (*Cruel, Cruel Love*), while in another he owned a motorcycle and was good for an elopement with a society girl (*The Jitney Elopement*).

In *Carmen* he appeared as Darn Hosiery, a Ruritanian hero, with brilliant improvisation in the dueling scene, during which he is at one moment bored and stands brushing his clothes, while at another he turns the fight into a ballet, a wrestling match, or a game of billiards, ending with a grand swing on suspended ropes of onions. What characterized Charlie on the screen, therefore, was not the fact that he was a down-and-out, a tramp — though he was frequently seen as unemployed or clinging ineffectually to some odd job — but his attitude to life in whatever circumstances he found himself. From the wholly burlesque image of the crook, the go-getter, the city slicker, even the female impersonator, or the intrusive, lighthearted mischief-maker of such films as *Laughing Gas, The Property Man* or *In the Park,* or the comic drunk of *Caught in the Rain, The Rounders,* and half-a-dozen other films, there emerged gradually the much more sympathetic figure, the increasingly romantic, lovelorn pursuer of girls. This romantic figure was to appear more and more in Charlie's earlier films, though many still kept to the harder line of burlesque in exploiting the comic jealousy of irate husbands or out-

raged wives. Beautiful as Keystone's Mabel Normand undoubtedly was, she was also a sophisticated comedienne out
to score hard-line comic effects; Edna Purviance was very
different; her height and her full figure seemed to emphasize a largely maternal relationship with her diminutive
partner. She was not so much an active participant in
comedy — since it took some while for Charlie to shape her
into an actress — as a beautiful object of devotion for
Charlie's emerging soul. This is evident in the two most
important films he made for Essanay, *The Bank* and *The
Tramp,* and in the film Essanay was to mutilate, *Police,* in
which Charlie, the ex-convict, makes what amounts to a
bitter attack on the hypocrisy of the pious reformer whom
Charlie sees rob a blind man. He is won back to virtue,
however, by the kindness of Edna whom, along with another
crook, he has tried to rob. She feeds him and pretends he is
her husband to foil the police. *Police* was Charlie's most
socially critical film so far.

The Bank retains elements of burlesque, but also moves
in the direction of high comedy and even drama. Charlie
emerges as a very real character, with strong feelings, a
human being in a human situation, a man with whom the
audience can fully identify. In a beautifully timed sequence,
he opens the film with his arrival at the bank in the early
morning, his promenade through it to its innermost vault,
which he swings open only to take out his janitor's mop and
pail. After this there is some Keystone tussling with the
mop, resting on Charlie's shoulder and swung around to hit
his rivals in the face. There is real romantic emphasis in
Charlie's secret love for the beautiful stenographer, Edna,
who is in love with the cashier who is also called Charlie.
The obvious misunderstanding which follows encourages
Charlie the janitor to put a modest bunch of flowers on
Edna's desk, which she merely throws away. Overcome by
this rejection, he huddles into the obscurity of a corner,

utterly dejected. The dream follows, the bank is being robbed, Charlie leaps into heroic action, defeats the robbers, rescues Edna, and becomes the hero of the hour. While embracing Edna he wakes up, only to find he is kissing the head of his mop. So the cashier prevails in real life, and Charlie, accepting the inevitable, picks up the dead flowers Edna has thrown away and goes back to his humble duties. Edna, statuesque and beautiful, is not required to perform more than the simplest pantomime, and everything is left to the emotional mood Charlie's romanticism inspires. The only laughter in the film is sympathetic, except for the odd moments of slapstick and violent action.

In a comment on his work contributed to *The Theatre* in September 1915 (and reprinted in *Focus on Chaplin*), Charlie claimed he was trying to derive more of his situations from real life and moving away from burlesque. The struggling figure in *Work,* he said, came from a sad spectacle he had seen in the street of a workman striving to push a two-wheeled barrow which was far too heavy for him; the handle kept lifting him into the air until eventually both he and the contents of the barrow spilled over. "Comedy is the most serious study in the world," he said. "I start out to find my characters in real life. . . . Generally the best situations . . . the funniest, will be an exaggeration of such action in real life that I have seen my counterpart pass through, but which was not at all funny in itself." He then explains in detail how *The Tramp* originated through his accidental meeting with a real hobo in San Francisco. "He was suffering a little from lack of food, and intensely from lack of drink." Charlie gave him food and drink in a bar, and watched the effect as "the irresponsible joy of life" emerged from him. The hobo talked about walking from place to place, about his misfortunes, his search for food in the countryside, his dealings with people, farmers, officials, everyone who held him in suspicion. Charlie watched him, his gestures, his facial expressions. Then he set about contriving the story for the film of the tramp in the countryside, and added to this his romance with a farmer's daughter. He spent three weeks making this two-reel film, the finest, most lyrical of his Essanay pictures. His perfectionist sense asserted itself; he says he rehearsed over fifty times some details of action or expression. His stock company, he says, was getting used to his methods of work, and filmmaking with them had become a great pleasure.

Charlie is a tramp, but a genteel one, paring his nails with the ferrule of his cane. He settles down to an elegant, very special little meal under a tree, but a gang of robbers disturbs the peace of the scene. Charlie manages with acrobatic alacrity to rescue Edna, a farmer's daughter, from their attempt to steal her money. As a reward, her father gives him a job on the farm, and he goes about it in a romantic daze, watering the apple trees with a watering can, pumping a cow's tail to get milk, or encouraging a yokel to lump heavy sacks by prodding him in the rear with a pitchfork. The robbers return, but Charlie again chases them off, though he is shot in the leg for his pains. Edna, however, looks after him, and the one-sided romance reaches its climax only to be dispelled when her handsome, real-life lover arrives. Charlie then becomes his archetypal self, writing a farewell note to his lost love, collecting his bundle, preparing sadly to leave this idyllic spot in which he no longer has a place. He goes off, alone once more, a small figure isolated in the straight, ruthless perspective of the empty road stretching to the horizon. Then suddenly his disconsolate walk livens into a jaunt — he shrugs away his sorrows, kicks up his heels, and ambles hopefully into the future as the shot (an iris-out) is reduced to a small circle enclosing his receding figure.

In these films Charlie's face becomes more sympathetically expressive. His nose twitches, as if his mustache were tickling, and his fastidious grimaces express a world of doubt and misgiving. The changes in his expression reveal comic dumbfoundedness, tongue-in-cheek triumph at getting away with murder, affected innocence twisting into a fatuous grin, a coy smirk at a nude statue, sudden laughter in moments of success, scowls of outrage when faced with evil opponents, or deadpan nonchalance when playing the drunk doing outrageous things. He smiles invitingly at pretty girls, assumes his genteel, butter wouldn't-melt-in-my-mouth expression when on his best behavior and out to impress. At romantic moments he looks boyishly hopeful. Although he still wears a slightly exaggerated eye makeup and outlined eyebrows, his face is left free, apart from the small mustache, to show whatever expression he needs to suggest his feelings. The art of facial expression was an essential part of his pantomime, and added to its growing subtlety. Charlie was educating himself in the art of comedy at the same time as he was educating the public. In this sense, the very gradual evolution of his style was fortunate rather than the reverse.

Far from outstripping public taste, his new films were in ever-increasing demand. Essanay was able to charge exhibitors a minimum rental of $50 a day for each film, while $50,000 had to be put up as an advance. When Charlie was offered $25,000 for a fifteen-minute appearance nightly for two weeks at the New Hippodrome in New York, Anderson gave him the $25,000 to turn the offer down. It was in 1915 that toys and miniature statuettes of Charlie began to be advertised, Charlie Chaplin squirt rings ("Here you are, boys"), and so forth. He received stacks of fan mail, and proposals for the use of his image in every kind of subsidiary form had to be dealt with. Sydney, still working at Keystone, became increasingly involved in the business side of Charlie's activities. He suggested to Essanay that the two-reelers should be marketed at a rate scaled to the size of the theater, so that each film might bring in $100,000 or more. Charlie realized that he was being vastly underpaid, and Essanay came forward with a $10,000 bonus for each completed film, and eventually made the very handsome offer of $350,000 for twelve two-reelers, the studio bearing all production costs. Charlie countered by asking for $150,000 bonus on signature. Spoor refused this, but Charlie did not care. His success, in his own words, was "bewildering, frightening — but wonderful."

When Sydney's contract with Keystone was completed, he took over Charlie's contractual arrangements while his brother finished the work for Essanay. Sydney traveled to New York to negotiate the best deal he could. As soon as Charlie had finished *Carmen,* he too went East, feted all the way when the news leaked out that he was on the train. Sydney met him in New York, tense with excitement. He had netted the deal of the century — $10,000 a week, and a bonus of $150,000 on signature. This was the offer made by the Mutual Film Corporation. Charlie was staggered, but also made to feel increasingly lonely in his amazing good fortune. All he felt like doing was to wander up Fifth Avenue hoping he might catch a glimpse of Hetty Kelly, who he knew was living with her married sister at number 834. He did not dare to go in. Later he stood in the crowd watching the news of his deal with Mutual put up on the roving electric sign that ran around the Times building. It was a strange, dual experience — he felt like a little man in the street looking at the good fortune of a big man in the news, but the big man was also himself. He was twenty-six, and assured now of becoming a millionnaire.

In making this offer, Mutual were in fact prepared to invest up to $100,000 in each of Charlie's forthcoming two-reelers; D. W. Griffith's three-hour epic, *The Birth of a Nation,* had cost only $110,000 when it was made the previous year. Charlie was now to become increasingly the perfectionist, and it was to take him eighteen months (with occasional time off) to complete the twelve two-reelers Mutual had expected to get inside a year, delivered at the rate of one a month. Even so, working at the Lone Star Studio in Lillian Way, Hollywood, Charlie created several half-hour masterpieces in the space of little more than a month each. These films remain among his most famous of the earlier period, and include such titles (made 1916–17) as *The Vagabond, One A.M., The Pawnshop, The Rink, The Cure, The Adventurer* and, best of all, *Easy Street* and *The Immigrant,* which served most of all to carry him forward. He managed to keep several of his stock players with him, including Leo White, Lloyd Bacon, John Rand, James T. Kelly, Charlotte Mineau and, of course, Edna Purviance. He added others, who were to stay with him after his Mutual contract was finished, notably Albert Austin, a former Karno actor, and Henry Bergman, who later became his assistant director and worked with him until his death in 1946. Eric Campbell, who in addition to being a Karno performer had played in Gilbert and Sullivan operas for the D'Oyly Carte Opera Company and retained his heavy, Mikado-like makeup in the films, took on the "Goliath" parts — most notably, the bully in *Easy Street.* Unhappily, he was to be killed in a car accident in 1917. Charlie also took his cameraman, Rollie Totheroh, over to Mutual.

In some of these films, Charlie kept close to tradition, but by having more time he was able to concentrate on technical improvements. Also he shot and reshot to achieve perfection. The slapstick becomes much more refined, combining acrobatics and ballet. The sets and properties have a far more solid and finished look to them compared with those of the Keystone and Essanay films. The films depending largely on adroit movement and comic gags worked out with objects were *The Floorwalker* (May 1916, with magnificent use of an escalator), *The Fireman* (June 1916, with comic business with a fire engine), *The Count* (September 1916, with much byplay on a slippery dance floor), *The Rink* (December 1916, with Charlie at his most graceful and agile as an expert on roller skates). Of these perhaps *The Count* was the most inventive, with its comic exploitation of a pretentious, overornate bourgeois setting and Charlie's David-versus-Goliath battles with Eric Campbell involving much surreptitious back-kicking during the dance sequences worked into the rhythm of the movement on the slippery ballroom floor. The polished dance floor provides the surface for the acrobatic chases at the end, Charlie's legs skidding on one spot with the rotations of a dervish. The roller skating in *The Rink* provides equal opportunities for comic grace and agility of movement. Charlie claims in his autobiography that no one was injured in his films, the movements were too carefully rehearsed and "treated like choreography." Only once, in *Easy Street,* did the head of the street lamp break off and give Charlie a severe cut on the nose.

Other films, while equally acrobatic in style, had more developed stories and touches of characterization, notably *Behind the Screen* (November 1916), a lightly satirical burlesque on slapstick filmmaking, and *The Adventurer* (October 1917). In *Behind the Screen* Charlie, called David, and Eric Campbell, called Goliath, are stagehands in a film studio making slapstick films. Edna, who wants to be an actress, disguises herself as a boy and becomes a stagehand too. When an actor quits because he regards pie-throwing as too highbrow, Charlie gets the job, but dodges all the pies which Goliath and others working on a serious film nearby receive in his place. The climax is the usual mayhem when Charlie does everything he should not, including being caught by Goliath kissing Edna, whom Goliath still supposes to be a boy ("Oh, you naughty boys!"). In *Behind the Screen,* too, Charlie gathers a mass of chairs on his shoulders and arms until he looks like a walking porcupine, and at the meal break chews meat from his neighbor's bone when it sticks out far enough for him to gnaw it. *The Adventurer,* with Charlie as an escaped convict, starts with one of the most brilliantly organized chases, Charlie tripping the cops and sliding between their legs. Elaborate circumstances lead him to become a guest at a wealthy woman's house party, with adventures such as dropping ice cream down the bare back of an elderly lady. When his true identity is discovered and the police arrive, there is a wild chase, in which Charlie momentarily disguises himself as a lampstand.

Apart from their technical skill and superior presentation, these films do not really advance Charlie beyond his Essanay days. *One A.M.* (August 1916) is also the perfecting of traditional work, rather than an advance. It is a sheer *tour de force* of inebriation, a solo performance based on almost ten years' experience in playing the comic drunk. The large entrance hall to the mansion where Charlie lives presents a maze of hazards: a large open space with a slippery floor covered with rugs (two of them animal skins with raised heads), a round table in the center with a rotating top on which a decanter offers further opportunity to drink, twin staircases with each side leading to a balcony above, on which there is a large stuffed bear and a wall clock with a massive swinging pendulum. Finally, there is a tall hatstand by means of which Charlie reaches the balcony precariously — when he finds, after several attempts, that the staircases are too much for him. The second half of the film takes place in the bedroom where a rotating, folding bed inset in the wall causes every trouble that may be imagined. The bed assumes a devastating energy of its own — trapping him, throwing him, tricking him. The whole setting of his home becomes a kind of nightmare with which he is totally unable to cope. In the end he collapses into the bathtub to sleep. Charlie plays the whole act in slow time, with deliberate, dignified movements, proceeding from object to object, and tangling in turn with everything.

Outstanding among the more conventional films for Mutual was *The Pawnshop* (October 1916), which showed at its finest Charlie's capacity for continual, inventive miming within the simplest of situations. As an assistant in the shop, he acts as the rival of another assistant for the attention of the boss's daughter, and has difficulties with the boss himself. He is fired and reinstated, and finally foils a thief in a climax of balletic energy. The film offers a continuous stream of imaginative byplay inspired by anything to hand — a balancing act on a pair of tall steps while cleaning the golden balls displayed outside the shop; the lightning movements by which he attacks his rival (with sudden, comic reversals of the situation); his use of the doughnuts as dumbbells, his tightrope walk on a length of recalcitrant rope, and above all his surgical dissection of a would-be client's alarm clock. *The Pawnshop* represents the height of Charlie's art in its earlier phase, the climax of his work as it developed at Keystone and Essanay.

But he had been for some while increasingly concerned to infiltrate new values into his work, something to satisfy the emotionalism deep in his own nature. Laughter alone was not enough for a man so emotionally committed. He had begun in *The Tramp* the previous year to experiment successfully in giving the tramp character, the "little fella," as he came to be called, an increasing identity in his own right, an identity which, although not wholly that of Charlie himself, could nevertheless be closely aligned with his own needs for self-expression. This emerged in varying degrees in the films of 1916–1917, in *Easy Street* (January 1917), *The Immigrant* (June 1917), and more particularly in *The Vagabond* (July 1916).

Easy Street is really Kennington in a nondescript, American guise. It could, in fact, be Any Street in an urban slum. Charlie is down-and-out, but soon reformed from a tendency to petty crime by his visit to the Hope Mission and the sight of the pastor's beautiful daughter. Inspired by a new spirit to do good, he joins the police force of Keystone-like cops, and clears the district of crime, overcoming the Goliath of the area (Eric Campbell) in a combat of agility against bullying bulk which occupies much of the film. There is a great deal of Keystone-Essanay left in this half-hour comedy with its excellently constructed story, and Charlie, half lost in a uniform many sizes too large, is for most of the time the knockabout clown, marvelous in the chase through doors and windows and up and down stairs, and balletic in his battles with the army of local crooks. But the impression left by *Easy Street* as a whole is by no means one of unalloyed burlesque — there are also the initial discovery of the tramp huddled and hopeless outside the mission, the glimpses of the underfed children in the slums, the mother who steals to feed her children and faints from starvation (Charlie's response being to steal more on her behalf), and the interesting introduction (uncensored at this period) of the quite realistic dope addict who assaults Edna, though his hypodermic is later used for comic effect when it accidentally invigorates Charlie and turns him into superman. The film, too, is extremely violent, much of it certainly burlesque, but enough rubs off (such as the bully's attack on his wife) to give the film an overall sense of realism, enhanced by the general excellence of the sets, especially that of the street itself. Some commentators have gone so far as to suggest the film involves actual social criticism, attacking the hypocrisy of the do-good workers at the Mission, since apart from Edna they are seen as mildly comic. But the atmosphere of the film is not so much consciously critical of society (in the sense that Charlie's later films were to become) as an exposure of what poverty, starvation, and violence look like, with comedy and burlesque introduced in a community derived from real life, much as Charlie had known it during his childhood.

The Immigrant has a greater proportion of human drama and a far stronger feeling of pathos. Again, the motivating force is poverty, affecting both Edna and Charlie, who are immigrants crammed with others into the steerage area of the ship arriving in the "Land of Liberty." Charlie's relationship with Edna and her mother is cemented by his relieving their distress after they have been robbed of their few savings by putting his winnings from a crap game into her pocket. Irony is introduced when the ship passes the Statue of Liberty and the passengers are treated like cattle. A romantic reunion occurs much later in a cheap restaurant where Charlie hopes to buy some food with a coin he finds but immediately loses through a hole in his pocket. (In any case, when the coin eventually reappears, it is counterfeit.) But on the strength of the coin he believes to be still in his possession, he orders a meal for himself and the girl, whom he treats with romantic gallantry. A poignant moment comes when Charlie learns that the girl's mother has died. An encounter with a rich artist, who asks them both to act as models, enables the couple to marry on a two-dollar advance — a romantic end being given to this film as it was to *Easy Street,* though, as Charlie puts it, the immigrants marry on a doleful, rainy day. The mood, he says, was set for him by the "wistful, tender" tune of an old song called "Mrs. Grundy." But in both films Charlie wins his girl. Although there is comic byplay both on the ship and in the restaurant — a marvelous continuity of incident, filled with tension, surrounding the loss and recovery of the coin, and final disillusion when Eric Campbell bends it with his teeth — once again the overall atmosphere is the meaning of poverty and the realities of suffering. Charlie the tramp emerges as an engaging, sympathetic human being as well as being a clown with ingenious sleight of hand when caught in some difficult situation. Charlie is said to have spent four days and four nights without rest cutting this film to his satisfaction.

The Vagabond goes even further in its romantic pathos — some say, too far — once Charlie, a tramp musician, gets away from the saloon in town to the countryside. Here he befriends a lonely girl by playing the violin, and then rescuing her from the bullying gypsies for whom she drudges. They set up camp together, but the girl's affection turns in the direction of a handsome artist who asks to paint her portrait. When the picture is exhibited, a wealthy woman declares the girl to be her long-lost daughter, and takes her away from Charlie. The film was given alternative endings: a romantic one in which true love prevails and the girl insists on returning in her mother's car to claim him, and a burlesque end in which Charlie, attempting to drown himself, is so horrified by the formidable appearance of the country woman who manages to save him that he dives straight back again into the water. There is almost no lighthearted comedy in this film — his scattering of the gypsies is more balletic than actual, and there are small jokes such as his raking up of the straw heap which has been his bed outside the caravan in which Edna has slept, or offering her the rake to remove the fleas from her hair, which he later washes himself ruthlessly and efficiently. But the comedy is laced with pathos, as so often in the later films. While she is away with the artist, he lays the table for their meal, using a shirt for a tablecloth on an upturned metal bath, the sleeves neatly folded up to make napkins. Again, what remains in the memory is the pathos rather than the comedy, such as the long look, repeated twice,

which Charlie gives the girl when, completely unconscious
of him, she stares after the departing artist, her smiling face
all too expressive of her admiration.

By 1917 Charlie's fame was such that he was faced by
imitators not only in the States but in other countries. This,
combined with the gross misuse of his early work over which
he had no direct control (prints circulate to this day in the
most mutilated form, since the negatives no longer exist and
the positives are used for duping, whether they are as originally cut or not) was to drive him, as soon as possible, to
become his own producer with permanent possession of his
work. At least he could then preserve it from being mutilated
and recut by alien hands. But he was not able to do much
about his imitators, such as Billy West, except show himself
to be far better than they were. Other imitators appeared
in Mexico, France and Germany; even Harold Lloyd admitted that he derived some of his initial comedy act
from him.

Charlie made a further, incredible step forward to ulti-
mate independence with his next deal. He turned down the
million dollars offered to him by Mutual for a further
twelve films, and signed in June 1917 with First National
for a million (plus $15,000 on signature) for eight films with
a minimum length of 1,600 feet (that is, something over
twenty minutes at silent speed) and with more money
($15,000 per reel) for any film running over 2,300 feet (that
is, over thirty-five minutes or so). The difference between
this contract and Mutual's offer meant that he was to become his own producer, bearing the production costs of
his films, whereas Mutual would have paid him the million
dollars as a fee and met the production costs as well. But
Charlie preferred to move in the direction of full control
which the First National contract represented. Another in-
ducement was that he would be able to acquire his own

studio rather than work in one controlled by his employers. He bought for $34,000 a five-acre lot in the Hollywood area between De Longpre Avenue, La Brea Avenue, and Sunset Boulevard, and built there an open-air stage (later to be roofed over), a house, and an administrative block designed (rather sentimentally) to resemble a row of English Tudor cottages.

One of the results of this move toward independence was that he slowed up his work considerably. The eight films he made for First National were to take him eight years to complete, yet the total reels of finished film they represented on the screen were approximately the same as the work he had completed for Mutual in eighteen months (twenty-five as against twenty-four reels, or some six hours of screen time). During 1917–1919 it took him approximately eighteen months to produce three films. He could afford the luxury of perfectionism which had already shown itself, for example, in his shooting ratio for *The Immigrant,* for which, according to Theodore Huff, he shot 90,000 feet in order to reach the finished print of some 1,800 feet, a ratio of about 50:1. He himself instances in an article written for *The American Magazine* (November 1918) that he sometimes shot as much as 60,000 feet to achieve 2,000 on the screen. Mack Sennett would have been utterly horrified at this, to him, appalling waste of film stock.

As we shall see later, Charlie's private life was to cause him much distress and distraction during this period. This included his brief, unhappy marriage to Mildred Harris, which took place in October 1918, and was followed by separation and finally by divorce in November 1920. The intense concentration he needed for his work was dissipated by anxiety and the effects of adverse publicity. As he says in the autobiography, he only got his ideas for films "by sheer perseverance to the point of madness," picking a subject that stimulated him, elaborating and evolving it, always discarding it if it did not develop to his fullest satisfaction. "Elimination from accumulation is the process of finding what you want." Mildred Harris, aged only sixteen at the time of her marriage, was quite incapable of understanding a husband as moody and demanding as Charlie during this crucial stage in his career.

In spite of his domestic troubles, during this unhappy period he was to complete two three-reel masterpieces, *A Dog's Life* (April 1918) and *Shoulder Arms* (October 1918); one three-reel experimental film in a new vein, *Sunnyside* (June 1919); a lesser film, *A Day's Pleasure* (December 1919), and one of his finest films, the six-reel feature, *The Kid* (February 1921). Apart from *The Pilgrim* (February 1923), this represented by far his best work for First National.

Charlie made no secret of the fact that he wanted to give the films and their characters a greater depth. In an analysis of his approach to humor which appeared in the same article already quoted (*The American Magazine*, November 1918), he made a number of basic points about his films. "All my pictures are built round the idea of getting me into trouble and so giving me the chance to be desperately serious in my attempt to appear as a normal little gentleman. . . . Always I try to contrast my seriousness of manner with the ridiculousness of the incident." Much comedy depends on misfortune visited upon the pompous, the pretentious, the authoritarian, or the unpleasantly rich, all of whom the average member of the audience resents. The policeman, heavy symbol of authority, is opposed by the "light and acrobatic" Charlie, who is always bullied by very big men. "The little fellow in trouble always gets the sympathy of the mob. Knowing that . . . I always accentuate my helplessness," wrote Charlie.

Owing to his small stature, the people in the audience want to mother or protect him. As for the tramp character, his clothes and his cane are all symbolic of the dapper little

Englishman, but one fallen into destitution. This was a matter of contrast, which Charlie says he regarded as an element in humor. He instances that he had to find a great six hundred-acre farm to point up the gag in *A Dog's Life* of planting the seeds one-by-one, by hand. Surprise is another element, doing the unexpected; and he instances the opening of *The Immigrant,* when he is seen back-view leaning over the side of the ship as if he is being violently seasick, when in actuality he is about to hook a fish. He concludes by saying how much he disliked the crude slapstick and horseplay of his early Keystone days. Now he avoids all such excess; he prefers, he says, restraint.

Charlie shared his concept of humor, as he claims in his autobiography, with his friend Max Eastman, whose book *Enjoyment of Laughter* was to be published much later in 1937. It is at this stage in his memoirs that he refers to Eastman's idea that comedy derives from "playful pain," and that there is much about it which is masochistic. Eastman was to quote from his conversations with Charlie, in which Charlie said:

> It seems to me that there are two different kinds of laughter. Superficial laughter is one escape. The waiter comes in and the duck isn't properly cooked, and you pick it up and throw it at him — yes, and by God, he throws it back! That's an escape. . . . That's superficial humour, slapstick. Subtle humour shows you that what you think as normal, isn't. This little tramp *wants* to get into jail. The audience thinks at first that he is ridiculous. But he isn't. He's right. The conditions are ridiculous. If I make them laugh that way, it's what I call subtle laughter.

This compares with Charlie's statement in his autobiography. Humor, he says, lies in:

> the subtle discrepancy we discern in what appears to be normal behaviour. In other words, through humour we see in

what seems rational, the irrational; in what seems important, the unimportant. . . . Because of humour we are less overwhelmed by the vicissitudes of life. It activates our sense of proportion and reveals to us that in an over-statement of seriousness lurks the absurd.

Eastman regarded Charlie as a man who "possesses a kind of perfection — a grace, poise and agility both of body and speech, that you are not moved to improve upon." He found him extremely serious; "instead of a funny man, he is a man of humorous imagination, the most original, perhaps, since Mark Twain, and also a consummate actor. . . . He is a poet of humour."

Max Linder, the French comedian to whom Charlie had already expressed his indebtedness, was for a while employed at Keystone in 1917, but failed to make any real comeback in films. He was suffering from war injuries, and his style of comedy, the debonair man-about-town getting into scrapes, was scarcely the Keystone style. After he had returned to France, he wrote in 1919 of Charlie, "It is impossible to get any idea of the continuous, highly intelligent effort of Charlie Chaplin in his work. He calls me his teacher, but for my part I have been lucky to get lessons at his school. . . . He works with the camera with the minutest care . . . but the secret is not in the mechanical work. . . . Charlie has studied laughter with care, and knows how to provoke it with the rarest precision. He leaves nothing to the chance of improvisation. He goes over and over scenes until he is satisfied. He 'shoots' every single rehearsal and has them thrown on the screen several times, so that he may find just the flaw which spoils the effect he is striving after." Linder records that Charlie had spent two months and 36,000 feet of film making a single 1,800 foot two-reeler, every scene shot twenty times as a result of some fifty rehearsals. "Before knowing him I was only his warmest admirer. Today I am his friend," he declared.

The French critic Louis Delluc, in his pioneer study of Charlie published in 1922, also quotes from an article written at this time by Elsie Codd, Charlie's secretary, emphasizing the advance work Charlie put into his films, preparing every movement, though "he never works with the help of his script." She emphasized the need to understand his moods during the difficult period of gestation:

> Before the great idea comes there is always a long succession of bad-tempered days and troubled nights. His more circumspect friends keep a respectful distance. . . . Once his decision is taken he . . . gets his friends together and tells them of his intention. . . . His great concern is now to get it realized. . . . No delay is tolerated.

Until the sets are built to his satisfaction, he seems "almost brokenhearted" at being held up. Work starts in his studio at nine o'clock; then the players and technicians are told what the day's work is to be.

> Once things have begun, Charlie's transformation is complete. All the preoccupation he may have been under disappear, and to all about him he is like a happy child enjoying some astonishing game of pretending. . . . Without exaggeration I think I can say that he has played every character in every one of his comedies.

Rehearsal means work and demonstration with every actor involved in turn, Charlie commenting, arguing, criticizing until he gets what he wants. He urges them not to "act," to aim at sincerity. He devotes the same care to the camera. Often the footage shot in a day is equal to that of the finished film. His secretary quotes a ratio of ten to fifteen feet to one finally used.*

* It is interesting to compare this account of Charlie at work in 1919 with that given in Kevin Brownlow's book, *The Parade's Gone By,* which describes in similar detail Charlie directing *A Countess from Hong Kong* almost half a century later.

In his autobiography, Charlie says that his next film, *A Dog's Life,* was much more carefully structured than he considers his previous films to have been. A half-length feature of three reels, its story flows from incident to incident, in which the human beings are treated just like the stray dog. Charlie rescues the mongrel from a dog fight with animals much bigger than itself; then a girl in a similar predicament has also to be rescued. The tramp is now a development of Pierrot, but the problem in these later, more realistic films was to motivate the beautiful heroine's romantic interest in the tramp. What they seem to experience is sympathy or pity for him, and this is usually mistaken by him for love, as in *The Gold Rush.* In *City Lights* he was to make the heroine blind.

But in *A Dog's Life,* the girl's situation was too desperate for the placidly beautiful Edna to be critical of the small and sympathetic tramp who befriends her. At the beginning of the film Charlie faces the cold dawn trying to sleep in a corner on waste ground. He stuffs a hole in the derelict fence to stop the draught and uses an old drainpipe for a muff. He steals food from a hot-dog stand through the hole in the fence, but hastily returns it when the huge form of a cop looms into sight. There follows a game of hide-and-seek with the law, skilfully timed, with Charlie dodging around and rolling backward and forward under the fence. Meanwhile, Scraps, the "thoroughbred mongrel" is asleep in a discarded washing-up bowl. Charlie, having escaped the police, hurries to an employment office, but is always last in the line of men who run to the little windows where officials offer odd jobs to the crowd of unemployed. Charlie rushes from point to point like a starving dog. Scraps meanwhile finds food in the road, but much larger dogs fall on him and drag it from his mouth. Charlie dives into the howling mob of dogs and lifts Scraps clear, escaping himself with difficulty. The only thing they can find to consume is half a bottle of milk; Charlie dips Scraps's tail into the milk and encourages him to suck it. Charlie then distracts the keeper of a food stall (Syd Chaplin) while Scraps steals sausages; then in a brisk sequence for timing, Charlie snatches cookies, one-by-one, as the stall-keeper momentarily turns away. But once again, he is foiled by the cop.

That night they go to the Green Lantern café, the dog stuffed in Charlie's pants, his tail wagging through a hole in the seat. There is much comic business with the orchestra and on the dance floor, but Charlie is soon thrown out, though not before he has seen the girl of his dreams. She works at the café, where she is bullied by the proprietor, from whose clutches she is trying to escape. There follows a succession of events — Scraps discovers a stolen wallet hidden by two crooks and Charlie takes it back to the café. Now he can buy food. He promises to rescue Edna, who has been fired without pay for the work she has done. But the crooks, who are also waiting at the café, see the wallet and once again Charlie is humiliated and thrown into the street along with Edna. But, thoroughly aroused to retaliate, he returns and in a brilliant pantomime sequence outwits the crooks by hiding behind a curtain at the back of their table, stunning one of them, and putting his own arms into the stunned man's coat sleeves from behind, claiming his share of the money in dumb show. He gets it eventually, though not without a final scrimmage in which the wallet is tossed from hand to hand until it is at last caught by Scraps, who darts off with it. The idyllic close to the film sees Charlie, Edna and Scraps (with puppies) living happily in the countryside, where Charlie is starting a new career for himself in farming, poking holes in the ground of a field which stretches out behind him to the horizon. He is putting in the seeds one-by-one.

This film had all the direct simplicity and universality of a fable, and it is appropriate to regard it as a work of art rather than as an essay in social criticism, which is what too many commentators feel urged to do with Charlie's work the moment they sense a cue. The film is at once harsh and sentimental, sharp and sweet. The irony and the strong vein of humor running through it save it from any taint of sentimentality. The end title, "When dreams come true," introduces a quite logical happy ending. The opening sequence of the film, indeed right up to the café sequence, in which comedy and burlesque predominate, are a near perfect blend of laughter with a wholly realistic observation of the meaning of a life in which destitution, hunger and unemployment predominate. There is no sermon, no message even in this film and the censor, had he existed at this time in Hollywood, would no doubt have objected to the end. For Charlie and Edna's good fortune stems from stolen property, property which Charlie (remembering, no doubt, the rich haul of guineas which had once gladdened his mother) would no doubt claim the rich owed to the destitute.

If *A Dog's Life* raised still further Charlie's status as a filmmaker, this was advanced again by *Shoulder Arms*, which was released on the eve of the armistice and caught the public mood at the very moment people were ready to laugh at misfortune now happily just passed. The strength of this film, another half-length feature of three reels (originally intended to be five, as Charlie explains in his memoirs), was the realistic eye, expressing irony without bitterness, that it cast on the plight of the men in the trenches — their common emotions epitomized in Charlie's diminutive figure. He is incredibly garbed in uniform and hung about with the paraphernalia of a man at war, including a rat trap and a cheese grater for back-scratching. He ekes out existence in waterlogged trenches and, in dream only, achieves fantastic feats. At drill, however, he is naturally the odd man out, his bottom protruding, his big feet turned both in and out, by far the smallest man in a platoon of men of very varied size. Once in the trenches, his huge pack jams in the narrow entrance to the dugout until he is finally booted into the interior by his sergeant. Meanwhile, in the German trenches the men in a similar plight are being bullied by an arrogant, goose-stepping little officer. There is little to choose between either side. The common man always loses out.

When the letters from home arrive, there is nothing for Charlie, who contents himself, in a celebrated sequence, with miming his reactions to the sentiments expressed in another man's letter which Charlie reads over his shoulder. In a handout of food parcels, Charlie gets a dog biscuit and a cheese so rotten he has to put on his gas mask and toss it over to the German lines, where it lands slap on the little officer — a refinement of Keystone and the custard pie. When he goes to sleep in the dugout after rain, the hole in the ground is awash, and the sergeant's head (Sydney's) is only just above the waterline as he sleeps in his bunk. A candlestick floats on the surface of the water. Charlie, sleeping in the lowest bunk, has to fix up a phonograph horn and rubber tube to breathe as he settles down to sleep out of sight beneath the water.

In the next sequence, Charlie goes over the top, captures fifteen men, explaining on his return, "I surrounded them." Charlie is now a hero, the sergeant's respected friend, pulverizing the enemy and chalking up his score as if on a billiard marker; eating excellent food delicately, complete with wine, the neck of the bottle conveniently opened up by a passing German bullet. The first to volunteer for a dangerous mission, we see him next in no-man's-land disguised as a tree and knocking out soldiers with his arm in a branch when he is threatened with being chopped down for firewood. He is discovered and chased by a fat German, who gets himself jammed in a drainpipe through which Charlie passes with ease. Charlie escapes and finds an opportunity to sleep in a ruined house whose owner, a French girl (Edna), tends him after he has mimed to her the stars and stripes to show he is in the American army. When the fat German and others arrive with a large gun, Charlie escapes again, leaving the ruined house to collapse on the enemy. He is separated from the girl, who is captured. Charlie's final heroics involve no less than penetrating German Army headquarters, rescuing the girl, and disguised as a German arresting the Kaiser himself, also played by Sydney. But the whole heroic action is, of course, a dream. Charlie wakes up to discover he is still a trainee, still the odd man out in the squad.

Charlie himself was strangely enough dubious of the film, indeed so uncertain that he came near to discarding it in spite of all the money and effort it had cost him. According to Charlie, it was rescued from destruction (or withdrawal) by the enthusiastic response to its humor of Charlie's closest friend, Douglas Fairbanks, Sr. The film was, in fact, extremely successful. The comic invention of the last section in the German headquarters, as happens sometimes in Charlie's longer films, shows a certain decline in invention, making the more imaginative climax of the film the tree sequence and the subsequent chase. The character of the "little fella," too, is far more developed in the earlier sequences of the film than in the last section, when he is largely concerned to carry through the action.

Charlie's next film, *Sunnyside* (June 1919) — an undertaking which, during his marriage difficulties, was, he says, "like pulling out teeth"— was nevertheless different to the point of sheer experiment. There is little actual laughter in it, far more daydreaming in a pastoral, idyllic atmosphere; its climax being the dream ballet in which Charlie plays Pan in his burlesque but beautiful dance with the wood nymphs. Charlie had first met Waslaw Nijinsky when the

In *The Champion* (1915)

In *The Pawnshop* (1916)

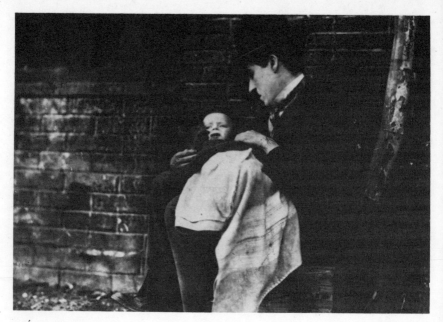

In *The Kid* (1921)

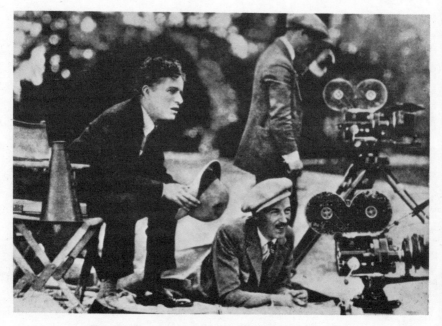

Chaplin directs a scene for *A Woman of Paris* (1923)

In *The Gold Rush* (1925)

In *The Circus* (1928)

With Paulette Goddard in the closing scene from
Modern Times (1936)

With Paulette Goddard in *The Great Dictator* (1940)

With Margaret Hoffmann in *Monsieur Verdoux* (1947)

great danger had paid a prolonged visit of two days to the studio during the winter of 1916–17. Charlie was making *The Cure*. "Your comedy is balletique, you are a dancer," he had said, and when Charlie had visited the Diaghilev Russian Ballet later that week, Nijinsky had insisted on talking to him in his dressing room during the intermission and keeping the audience waiting. "He was hypnotic, god-like, his sombreness suggesting moods of other worlds," writes Charlie. In *L'Après-midi d'un faune* he suggested "the tragic unseen lurking in shadows of pastoral loveliness." Six months later Nijinsky went insane.

Sunnyside is Charlie's response to the admiration expressed by Nijinsky. The film was not greatly appreciated at the time, though Louis Delluc in France was loud in its praise. In the main action Charlie, bullied by his boss, is the overworked odd-jobs man in a rural farmhouse, which appears also to be the local hotel. Charlie is the figure of pathos, in love with the village belle, unable to look after the livestock; riding on the back of a cow, he is tossed off, becomes unconscious and has his dream, dancing like Nijinsky until his movements are suddenly accelerated by contact with a cactus. The end is a happy one; the passing city slicker, who for a while puts Charlie in the shade in the eyes of the village belle, leaves for good, much as the city artist did in *The Vagabond*. Charlie's attempt at suicide in this film is yet another dream; dreams were to become a recurrent motif in his work.

A Day's Pleasure (December 1919) was a two-reeler, a relative interlude in his work. The title is an ironic reference to the misadventures of Charlie the family man taking his wife and two children out for a day at the seaside, with gags (in the traditional style, but developed amusingly) arising out of the car engine which stops and starts at its own and not the driver's will, hot tar on the road, the deck chair which collapses, seasickness, and so forth. Charlie goes back to being the victim, with little will to retaliate.

Over a year was to pass before audiences for Charlie's richer style were to be revived by another masterpiece, *The Kid* (February 1921). *The Kid* was Charlie's first feature-length film, being six reels, and represented a return to form after the two previous films. Charlie's search for a new sub-ject became increasingly agonized in the circumstances of an unhappy marriage, but, as he recreates the period in his memoirs, it was the sight of the four-year-old Jackie Coogan appearing on stage with his father, an eccentric dancer, and doing a few steps himself, which brought ideas flooding into his mind.* His father agreed to the child's working with Charlie, and Jackie proved unusually receptive to instruc-tion in acting. He could, writes Charlie, "apply emotion to the action and action to the emotion." And he could repeat the work without losing spontaneity, an essential quality for anyone engaged in Charlie's films. He had marked per-sonality, and the love he developed for Charlie showed very clearly in the film.

The introductory plot sequence shows a destitute girl ("Her only sin was motherhood") trying to do her best for her newborn baby. But circumstances lead the child to be left by crooks near a refuse bin in an alleyway. Here Charlie, once again the stylish tramp, discovers the baby. He re-peatedly tries to avoid taking any responsibility for it, but all his devices fail. He comes to care for it, and he takes it home to his garret. The humor derives directly from the situation, especially Charlie's efforts to take care of the

* This is Charlie's version of his discovery of Jackie. But Huff says he had already appeared in the crowd scenes of *A Day's Pleasure* in the autumn of 1919, prior to working through 1920 on *The Kid*, during which 500,000 feet of film were exposed for the approximately 6,000 feet used in the final version. Two cameras were brought in to create a second negative, for safety's sake.

baby's hygiene. Meanwhile, the maternal instinct has reasserted itself in the mother who, after a suicide attempt, faints when she realizes that her baby has completely disappeared.

Five years pass, and the main action begins. The tramp and the kid scrape out a living; the tramp mending the windows the kid breaks. The cops (recurrent in this film, as in others, as merciless authoritarians out to foil the little tricks by means of which Charlie hopes to survive) constantly intervene, but happiness for both of them comes when they are at home together in the garret, where the kid does the cooking and Charlie takes his ease, bringing up the child in polite ways. Charlie gets the worst of it in a street fight, and the plot reenters the action when the destitute girl, now a rich opera star, visits the slums but fails as yet to discover that the kid is her child. But authority intervenes to deprive Charlie of the child, and there is a near-horrifying scene when the County Orphan Asylum van arrives, and the kid and Charlie are separated by force. Charlie pursues the van on foot, frightens the driver away, and retrieves the kid. They go to sleep in a flophouse. By now, the opera star has evidence that the kid is her child, since a note she wrote and pinned to the baby's clothes when she abandoned him has been discovered in Charlie's possession. While Charlie sleeps, the flophouse owner steals the child in response to a reward offered by the mother in the press.

Charlie, alone now, dreams of heaven, the slum street and its denizens transmuted into angels, though a feathery fight takes place when devils enter and prompt Charlie to make advances to a girl angel which result in a jealous scrimmage. The cops in the dream are after him again, but he wakes to find a real cop in the act, as it seems, of arresting him. But it is no arrest. Charlie is being escorted to meet the grateful mother of "his" child.

The Kid fully establishes the line of Charlie's feature films of humane comedy, pathos, and social observation. The themes are love and humanity and companionship versus poverty, inhumanity, and the heartlessness of blind authority. Charlie's small, appealing figure is set against the bulk of the Bully, or the Cop, and the mean-minded official or bureaucrat. The loneliness and the vulnerability of the sympathetic characters finally draw them together in bonds of affection, and Charlie has to choose in each instance whether to end the film by himself, or in company with those he has loved. In the old days, he was content to pull out with an independent, jaunty air, overcoming a disappointment which was inevitable. Now, as the tramp character becomes less defiant and more pathetic, happy ends are in some cases permitted, as in *The Vagabond, Easy Street, The Immigrant,* and *A Dog's Life.*

The Kid, according to Huff, cost Charlie approximately $500,000 and almost eighteen months' work, and he forced First National to give him $600,000 for it, since his basic contract was for two-reelers. The film took $2.5 million, and Charlie earned over $1 million from it. As we shall see, his estranged wife attempted to attach the film during the divorce proceedings, and Charlie had to bolt overnight to Salt Lake City with some 400,000 feet of film during the process of editing.

It was during this period that Charlie joined in the consortium of top creative talent in Hollywood to form United Artists, which was established in April 1919. Mary Pickford and Douglas Fairbanks, Charlie and the director D. W. Griffith combined to produce and distribute their own films independently. Because of his contract with First National, Charlie was unable to reach complete independence before 1923; *A Woman of Paris* was to be his first production made entirely without commitment to any company but his own. The formation of United Artists came about partly as the result of a strong rumor that the main production companies were going to merge in order to exercise mutual control over the highly competitive and astronomical salaries demanded by such top stars as Fairbanks, Charlie, and Mary Pickford. The formation of United Artists was, therefore, a strategic move, and in Charlie's case, planned four years before he was free to take advantage of this full measure of artistic and economic independence.

Charlie's next two films for First National, *The Idle Class* (September 1921) and *Pay Day* (April 1922), were short, efficient two-reel comedies, which did not attempt any advance. Charlie, worn out by the worries of his divorce, left the studio just as he was due to start *The Idle Class,* and ran off in August 1921 on the first of his nostalgic tours of Britain and Europe (to be described later), only resuming production on his return in October. These two films are on the level of the Mutual two-reelers. In the first Charlie plays the dual roles of a rich but absentminded husband and a tramp in love with the rich man's neglected wife. In the final development of the plot, the wife (Edna) temporarily mistakes the tramp for her husband in disguise at a masquerade ball, while the husband is sealed up inside a suit of armor. The pathos here is thin, but the comedy strong. In *Pay Day,* Charlie is a worker on a building site; he is late for work, juggles bricks, and is in trouble with the foreman (Mack Swain), whose pretty daughter (Edna) he admires. But in reality he is married to a domineering wife (Phyllis Allen), and he must work to earn the money she insists on seizing from him. This film is both more ironic and more realistic than *The Idle Class.*

The final film for First National was *The Pilgrim,* a four-reeler featurette directed in the height of Charlie's style of the early 1920s. It was completed in September 1923, and left him free to work in his own time and in his own way,

distributing his work, which he now had to finance entirely
from his own resources, through the consortium of United
Artists.

For its period the film was daring in its burlesque of false
piety — so much so that it was for a time banned in the
state of Pennsylvania. It is essentially critical — of rural
puritanism; of the spoiled child (a character in marked
contrast to Jackie in *The Kid*). Charlie is an escaped convict, whose disguise as a minister (baggy black clothes, wide-
brimmed black hat) results quite accidentally from stealing
a minister's clothes. He sticks a pin in a list of places before
buying a railway ticket, and finds himself, on arrival at the
chance destination of Devil's Gulch, feted by a religious
group — a strange assortment of tall women and little men
— who are expecting a new minister and immediately accept
Charlie in place of the real man, whose message that he is
delayed Charlie, rising to the occasion, manages to intercept
and destroy. Charlie is now the prisoner of his disguise; they
all process to the chapel and Charlie then and there has to
improvise a service, which he does by taking his cue from
the sacristan. Charlie's sermon is his famous pantomime of
the fight between David and Goliath, which he turns into a
kind of theatrical performance. Charlie takes several "cur-
tains" and shows every desire to take the collection, too. The
congregation, except for a naughty boy, find the new
minister rather a puzzle.

The second part of the film moves from the chapel to the
lodging where the new minister is to live — the house of
Mrs. Brown and her beautiful daughter. The welcoming
party includes the naughty boy (played by Dinky Dean, son
of Chuck Riesner, the former boxer, Keystone writer, and
actor who became Charlie's assistant and associate director
from 1918 to 1925). The denouement develops following the
arrival of a crook who recognizes Charlie as the escaped
convict. Meanwhile, the naughty boy takes over the action;

he is uncontrollable, climbing all over Charlie and finally putting his father's bowler hat over the plum pudding before it is covered with sauce. Charlie, forgetting his clerical status, belts him in the stomach.

By now Charlie is in love with the daughter of the house, and he is determined to foil the crook, whose intention is to rob Mrs. Brown of the mortgage money she keeps by her. Charlie fails, so he goes out in pursuit of the crook and uses his nefarious skill to retrieve the money and return it to his landlady. But by now the Sheriff is searching for an escaped convict disguised as a pastor, and Charlie walks into his arms before he is able to return the money. Under arrest, he can only bid the girl a fond and frustrated farewell. Luckily for him, the Sheriff has realized that he is trying to go straight, so he conducts him to the Mexican border, urging him to "cross the line." But what with the lawless gunplay he sees going on in Mexico and the law enforcement he has to face in the United States, Charlie is quite unable to know what to do for the best. The film ends ironically with him running along the border, straddling it with a foot on both sides, hopping now to one, now to the other country as he makes his final departure.

The overall atmosphere of *The Pilgrim* is both ironic, humane, even at times tender — humane because the convict becomes essentially a good man (inspired, it is true, by his response to Mrs. Brown's daughter); tender in Charlie's embryonic love affair with the girl, and ironic because of its exposure of the hypocrisy of the officially "good" people (the deacon is discovered to be carrying homemade hooch in his pocket), and the virulence of the tricks of the naughty boy and the severity of the punishment he gets from Charlie. *The Pilgrim* was to be the last of Charlie's comedies until *The Gold Rush* of 1925, and it remains one of his best.

Charlie himself has explained the generation of his next film, his only tragedy though by no means his only "serious" film. He was now, as we have seen, a member of the United Artists group, and could decide the nature of his own productions, offering them for distribution through United Artists. His stock company of players for First National was now dispersed, all but Edna Purviance, who remained on the payroll, and to whom Charlie felt he owed some kind of gesture. In spite of their private estrangement, they remained friends, and Charlie's loyalty to her on the financial level was to be lifelong. Although she was only in her late twenties, she was inclined to look matronly, and she was no longer good casting in the comedies Charlie was beginning to envisage. His desire to try his hand at a serious, "psychological" film in which she might star as a "mature" actress led him to consider directing her in a version of *The Trojan Women,* or again as Josephine in a study of her relationship with Napoleon. However, significantly enough, Charlie became more absorbed in the possibilities of the character of Napoleon, "this flamboyant genius," to be played by himself, than in the personality of Josephine. But in any case the project fell through.

Another flamboyant character, the much married Peggy Hopkins Joyce (a girl of humble origin who enjoyed extracting fortunes from her succession of millionaire husbands) entered briefly into Charlie's life, and the entertaining stories this chic, bejeweled lady told him of life in Paris became the origin of the story idea for *A Woman of Paris,* a film in which Charlie looked forward, as he says in the autobiography, "to convey psychology by subtle action," "subtle suggestion," concentrating on the small, revealing details of situation and reaction. In this he virtually anticipated Lubitsch, or at least paralleled in Hollywood the Lubitsch "touch" which the German director was establishing in the so-called *Kammerspiel* films (chamber dramas) in Germany, and was soon to make in Hollywood, starting with *The Marriage Circle* (1924). Though only a success with the discriminating, sophisticated audiences of the period (it was released in October 1923), *A Woman of Paris* was an influential film, setting new standards of psychological observation though in a story of somewhat traditional, even melodramatic theatrical style.

It was a style Charlie was to maintain appealed to him, even if it might lead to accusations that his taste was old-fashioned. "To me theatricalism means dramatic embellishment . . . the abrupt closing of a book; the lighting of a cigarette; the effects offstage, a pistol shot, a cry, a fall, a crash; an effective entrance, an effective exit — all of which may seem cheap and obvious, but if treated sensitively and with discretion, they are the poetry of theatre." This is what he developed in terms of film for *A Woman of Paris,* in which he cast Adolphe Menjou (already an actor of some repute) to star opposite Edna, and who in fact stole the picture from her. It established his stardom but (in spite of hard work and worthy effort) it failed to establish hers.

The film took nine months to make, cost $800,000 of Charlie's own capital, and was edited from some half-a-million feet exposed in Charlie's studio. The story was developed somewhat in the tradition of *Camille.* Charlie called it a "drama of fate," and, in the style of the time, gave it a verbal preface on the screen: "Humanity is composed not of heroes and villains, but of men and women, and all their passions, both good and bad, have been given them by God. They sin only in blindness, and the ignorant condemn their mistakes, but the wise pity them." The characters therefore were not all good, not all bad, thus avoiding the popular novel formula of virtually all dramatic films of the early 1920s. They were mixed and uncertain in their motives. Nor did Charlie hedge about his characters' morals, veiling nothing, and he made no stringent moral comment on their behavior. He simply let the story run its course. Made with great restraint, the film ran through the succession of situations which led to the denouement.

Turned out by their parents, Marie and her artist-lover
Jean determine to run away, but through mischance Marie
leaves alone for Paris and is seen to become, by a rapid
transition, "a woman of Paris," the mistress of the suave and
wealthy Pierre Rivel. Rivel, however, is due to marry, and
relations are strained though he assures her his marriage
will make no difference to their association. Marie first
learns of the engagement through an announcement in a
magazine shown her by one of her friends — she lights a
cigarette to cover her emotion, the "Chaplin touch." Jean,
meanwhile, has set up as an artist in Paris; they meet again,
and Jean's desire for her remains as strong as ever in spite of
his mother's hostility. He agrees to paint her portrait, and is
torn between the rival pressures of his love for his mother,
and for Marie; after attempting to attack Pierre, he shoots
himself. Although his mother, in her grief, considers shooting Marie, they are in the end linked together in their
sorrow. The title reads, "Time is a great healer, and experience teaches us that the road to happiness is in the service
of others." Back in the country, the two women take to the
care of orphan children, and in the final shot, Pierre in his
luxurious car and Marie, seated on a haywagon, pass each
other without recognition. A second, more bitter and
sophisticated end was shot for distribution in Europe, in
which Marie, after Jean's suicide, goes back to Pierre.

Although the story, thus summarized, reads like a melodrama, and the titles sound moralistic, Charlie was in fact
dramatizing the situation with great restraint, suggesting
rather than emphasizing. Pierre is no villain, but a man who
thinks he gives as much as he takes from his mistresses, for
whom he has no real feeling. Marie's women friends in
Paris are treacherous, but human; in the celebrated mas-
saging scene, Fifi joyfully breaks her promise to Paulette
that she will not tell Marie she has seen her out with Pierre.

The Swedish girl masseuse avidly takes it all in; this is the only comedy touch in the film. Everything is presented on a normal, restrained level of action and reaction, except for the moments of violence. Even the shock of Jean's suicide is largely achieved through the reactions caused in the cabaret where he shoots himself. Charlie, perhaps wisely, has preferred latterly to let *A Woman of Paris* remain unseen. A seminal film in its time, it could well be that its reputation as a classic of the cinema might be strained if it were to be seen today, though its continuing unavailability is a disappointment for those studying the history of the cinema.

Charlie's pace of production slowed now to a single film every two years, and later to intervals of three to four years between each film, after the coming of sound to the cinema. *The Gold Rush* (August 1925), which he subtitled "a dramatic comedy," saw the return of Mack Swain (at $250 a week) as Charlie's principal partner. It also saw, after his removal of his second wife, Lita Grey (whom Charlie had married in November 1924), from the part of the unnamed girl, the engagement of Georgia Hale as the replacement for Edna Purviance as his leading lady.* His associate director

---

* Georgia Hale had appeared in a low-budget film directed by Josef von Sternberg, *The Salvation Hunters,* which Charlie helped to have distributed at the request of the English actor George K. Arthur. John Baxter in his book *The Cinema of Josef von Sternberg* claims that Georgia Hale, "brooding and self-destructive . . . is the prototype Sternberg heroine" in *The Salvation Hunters* (1925). She played opposite George K. Arthur, who had written and partly financed the film. Since Arthur knew Charlie, he asked him to view the film and help him get it distributed. "Charlie told me he thought we had the greatest picture ever," Arthur said. Douglas Fairbanks, equally enthusiastic, bought a quarter share in the film for "a sum exceeding many times the cost," and arranged distribution through United Artists. Charlie, having taken over Georgia Hale for *The Gold Rush,* later came to Sternberg's aid by inviting him to direct his next serious film after *A Woman of Paris, The Sea Gull (A Woman of the Sea),* which he had scripted for Edna Purviance. Sternberg alleged Edna Purviance had become an alcoholic and was unemployable. The film was shot on a Californian location in the Expressionist style. According to John Grierson, Charlie, who saw the film along with Grierson, insisted that Stern-

was Charles Riesner, and Harry d'Abbadie d'Arrast, who had advised on *A Woman of Paris,* stayed with Charlie as assistant director.

Charlie gave one of his very finest dramatic performances in this film, which many still consider to be his best, as it appears to be for Charlie himself, who has been recorded as saying that this was "the picture I want to be remembered by." The idea was inspired, he says, by looking at stereoscopic photographs of Alaska, the Klondike, and the gold prospectors, together with the grim story of the Donner expedition, which had led to disaster, starvation, and even cannibalism.*

The film was made without a script following the usual traumatic heart-searching for comic ideas, and production began in the spring of 1924, lasting fourteen months, while locations were set in the snow-covered mountains of Nevada. The costs soared in the direction of a million dollars, but in the end the film was so successful internationally that Charlie made more than two million dollars' profit. The film had a second lease of life in 1942, when he reissued it as a sound film, with music and narration spoken in his light, musical voice with its quick enunciation.

The Gold Rush works simultaneously on two levels. First, it is the story of two prospectors, Charlie (the Lone Prospector) and Mack Swain (Big Jim) in the Klondike in 1898. Second, it is the story of Charlie's need for love and companionship. Alone and lost in a violent storm, Charlie seeks

---

berg reshoot some sequences to emphasize the "sentimental humanism" in the script. The result satisfied no one, and the film was shelved. Grierson called this film "the most beautiful picture ever produced in Hollywood, and the least humane."

* Charles Fayette McGlashan's *History of the Donner Party* (1879) had been reissued in 1922, and many of the incidents in *The Gold Rush* parallel McGlashan's account of the tragic expedition of the 1840s; these include Charlie as the chicken (cannibalism), the introduction of the bear, and the eating of the moccasin (boot).

refuge in the cabin belonging to the villain, Black Larsen. The wind is so strong that it blows him in at one door and out at another. Big Jim also arrives, and after a fight, Larsen is subdued. Larsen kills two mounted police who are trailing him, and makes off with their sled. Left alone, the two starving men celebrate Thanksgiving with the only food available — one of Charlie's big boots. Big Jim becomes delirious with hunger and Charlie turns into a strutting chicken before his eyes. After a struggle, they part as friends. Big Jim then discovers that Larsen has stolen his claim; they fight and Big Jim is knocked unconscious, but Larsen dies in an avalanche.

Charlie, meanwhile, goes to town, and experiences romantic feelings for the vivacious dance hall girl, Georgia, who laughs at him with the other girls behind his back but uses him as a foil against the big handsome man who is pursuing her. Later, as a joke, she and her girl friends promise to come on New Year's Eve to a dinner in a cabin Charlie has been loaned. Charlie prepares as elegant a meal as his poverty permits, but Georgia and the others never arrive. Charlie has to dream that they are there, and he performs the "dance of the rolls" to entertain them. He dreams that Georgia kisses him. Then he wakes, and can only watch the New Year celebrations as a lonely outcast, with Georgia in the handsome man's arms. Georgia remembers her forgotten date, but only when it is too late.

Big Jim, his memory partially gone, is still searching helplessly for his lost claim; he rejoins Charlie. Together they look for and discover Larsen's cabin. Another storm blows the cabin onto a cliff edge, where it balances precariously — but as they escape, Charlie and Jim find the claim. The Epilogue follows: Jim and Charlie are millionaires returning to the States by ship and feted by the press. A happy end brings about the reunion of Charlie and Georgia, whom he finds traveling steerage in the same ship.

Like all Charlie's stories, *The Gold Rush* is a fable, each episode an enrichment of the underlying situation — poverty and hunger for men in dire straits and the basic human need for companionship and love. Although the film is laced throughout with a wonderful sense of humor, one is left with the overall feeling that it is a sad, not humorous, film with a somewhat contrived happy ending. It is as if Charlie could not bear to leave *The Gold Rush* without relieving its melancholy, much as Shakespeare's happy ends in the comedies often seem "contrived" in this sense. But if this film is accepted as a fable, and not as a story which (for all its moments of seeming realism) should conform to actuality, the happy end can be seen more as a comment than a contrivance — human beings can achieve happiness if they set out to do so.

Enrichment through humor is everywhere in *The Gold Rush* — the burlesque comedy of the storm blowing Charlie and Big Jim through Larsen's cabin; the comedy of hunger (Charlie eating a carefully salted candle like celery, and relishing his boot and its laces, with the pantomime of a gourmet); the comedy of delirium, with Charlie becoming a giant chicken chased by the famished Jim; the comedy of pathos in Charlie's exquisitely performed dance of the rolls which he enacts with changes of facial expression; the comedy of tension as the cabin teeters on the brink of destruction. This is not the comedy of the quick, superficial laugh, but the comedy of feeling; the humor that comes to relieve pain and help humanity to share its common burdens. *The Gold Rush* could be called at once Charlie's saddest and most humorous film, and this is probably the reason why he feels it to be his best, or at least the film for which he prefers to be "remembered."

After launching *The Gold Rush* in August 1925, Charlie began gestating his next film, the ill-fated production of *The Circus* (January 1928). Its conception, preparation and production ran parallel with his even more deeply troubled second marriage, the circumstances of which are considered later. He had married the sixteen-year-old actress Lita Grey (Lolita McMurry) in November 1924; separation finally followed in December 1926, and the painful litigation of 1927 interrupted actual production of the film, divorce being finally achieved in August 1927. Inasmuch as a miniature circus had to be established for the production of the film — which in the end lasted more than a year — costs ran up to little short of $1 million. *The Circus* was for the most part completed during 1926, but the final stages had to be abandoned until after the divorce settlement came through because ownership of the film became involved in the divorce litigation. A friend of Lita's, Merna Kennedy, was the leading lady, though Lita was eventually to turn against her through jealousy. Charlie discovered a new assistant director and leading actor in Harry Crocker, who played Rex, the conventionally handsome man, a tightrope walker, who deflects Merna's romantic interest from Charlie. Harry Crocker belonged to a wealthy family in San Francisco and had studied at Yale. Of the old team of the past, only Henry Bergman remained, who had joined Charlie in 1916, and was to remain with him as actor and general assistant until his death in 1946. He also ran a restaurant in Hollywood. *The Circus* has suffered unfairly by comparison with the perfection of *The Gold Rush*. The public, fortunately, liked it better than Charlie did; for him the film had melancholy associations, and he does not even mention it in his autobiography. He was less able to concentrate on *The Circus* than on any other of his major films and this was an agony for him. It is not surprising, therefore, that *The Circus* leaves the impression of melancholy and loneliness rather than of humor, and that there are occasional moments when it fails to hold the attention. But considered on its own individual merits, and not in comparison with *The Gold*

Rush or *City Lights,* it is still one of the finest films of the 1920s, and views well today. What it lacks, however, is the comedy-in-depth, the total poetic conception of *The Gold Rush*. It is memorable for moments which form highlights, like the incomparable sequence which ends the film: Charlie left alone, in the depths of isolation, sitting on an empty box on the waste lot as the circus wagons pass him by, an end implying total loss like that Garbo was to embody later at the end of *Queen Christina*. Charlie's emotion is conveyed by absolute stillness, absolutely concentrated restraint. But *The Circus* as a whole became a film of episodes, either comic or dramatic, which are strung together along the general story line.

The film begins with an extremely funny chase with a crook, a cop, and Charlie, mistaken for a thief, involved in a mirror maze, and Charlie's accidental intrusion into a vanishing lady act in a traveling circus. Charlie seems all set to become a natural comic, but his ambitions to become a clown fail when he attempts conventional clowning. But he stays with the circus as a prop assistant because he has fallen in love with a bareback rider (Merna), the victimized stepdaughter of the bullying circus proprietor, a purely stock villain. A belligerent donkey takes a dislike to Charlie, and their antics in public lead the audience to applaud. His newfound success gives Charlie fresh bargaining power with the proprietor, and enables him to protect Merna. But she is secretly in love with Rex, the tightrope walker, the large, handsome man who is always Charlie's formidable rival in love. One of the great moments in the film comes when Charlie deputizes for Rex on the high wire, a sequence for which Charlie put in months of training to make himself sufficiently expert to sustain the dangerous tricks he performs. But his attempts to protect Merna lead to his dismissal, and he sacrifices her to Rex, who marries her, and ensures her reconciliation with her stepfather. So the circus moves on without further need for Charlie, but after his moment of desolation, he waddles off towards the horizon, abandoning lost hopes with a shrug as he had so often done before.

Charlie was now faced with the most perplexing technical and artistic problem of his career: how to adjust to working in the medium of sound film, which was gradually being introduced to the cinemas of the world during the later 1920s. Charlie resented bitterly the inevitable coming of sound. In January 1931, three years after its establishment in American films and a few days prior to the release of *City Lights,* his next film, he contributed an article to the *New York Times* on pantomime and comedy, arguing that the nondialogue film represented a universal art which could not, or should not, be ousted by the current "hysteria" for talkies. Pantomime, he claimed, is a universal language, while speech as a form of communication is restricted to those who understand it. "Action is more generally understood than words," he said. "Pantomime lies at the base of any form of drama. . . . Pantomime is more important in comedy than it is in drama. . . . Most comedy depends on swiftness of action, and an event can happen and be laughed at before it can be told in words. . . . Pantomime, I have always believed and still believe, is the prime qualification of a successful screen player. . . . Consider the Irvings, Coquelins, Bernhardts, Duses, Mansfields and Booths, and you will find at the root of their art pantomime." The only thing Charlie welcomed when the sound track arrived was the fact that he could now compose and control the synchronized music, giving his films the "elegant and romantic" music he felt they needed, working in counterpoint to the comedy, but always being responsive to the sentiment.

City Lights (February 1931) was a synchronized film, "a comedy romance in pantomime," accompanied by music devised by Charlie himself, except for the theme tune, "La

Violetera" ("Who'll buy my violets?"), which his friend the Spanish singer Raquel Meller had sung on her tour of the States in 1926. In the autobiography, Charlie says that two themes he had had in mind motivated the film — a blind clown and his relationship with his small daughter, and an experiment made by two rich men of abducting a tramp while he was asleep, waking him, steeping him for a while in luxurious living, and then, when he was in a drunken stupor, returning him to the place where they found him. These themes merged in *City Lights,* but the blindness was transferred to the flower-seller, played by Virginia Cherrill, a beautiful socialite with few acting ambitions, the divorced wife of Irving Adler. Later she was to become the Countess of Jersey.

City Lights took two years to make and, according to Charlie, cost him two million dollars. Production began in March 1928, and was frequently interrupted because, for one reason or another, Charlie was dissatisfied. Virginia Cherrill proved unpunctual at the studio and difficult to coach, and at one stage, when the film was half shot, Charlie considered dismissing her and bringing back Georgia Hale. "This was not the girl's fault," Charlie admits in the autobiography; "I had worked myself into a neurotic state of wanting perfection." One by one his associates disappeared — Harry Crocker dismissed, Henry Clive (playing the millionaire) thrown out when his work was all but complete because he refused to fling himself into a tank of cold water. Some 800,000 feet of film were exposed for a comparatively short film, playing eighty-seven minutes only, representing some 9,000 feet. But the film enjoyed an astonishing success, proving all those wrong who had said Charlie was crazy to expect the public to come to see what was, in effect, a silent film in the new era of sound.

City Lights, like *The Gold Rush,* established a relationship in depth between the humorous and the pathetic.

There is also a sharpness added, Charlie's latent irony, the tough streak in his nature. The tramp inadvertently thumbs his nose at pomp when, during an unveiling ceremony, he is discovered asleep in the stony lap of a giant statue of a woman representing "Peace and Prosperity." He climbs into a position which makes him appear to be thumbing his nose at the dignitaries conducting the ceremony. After various comic moments in the city, the tramp, escaping from a cop by clambering through a parked limousine, inadvertently deceives a blind flower girl that he is the millionaire owner of the car. Discovering she is blind, and at the same moment lost in admiration for her beauty, he gives her his last coin. (This scene, says Charlie in the autobiography, took five days' repeated shooting to perfect.) After showing the girl in a garret with her grandmother, Charlie enters on one of the most beautifully contrived sequences in the film — his strenuous attempts to save the drunken millionaire from drowning himself. The rope gets around his own neck and he is nearly drowned instead; each man tries to save the other, and in the end, wet through, the millionaire takes the tramp home, plies him with unwanted drink, and drags him out on the town, which results in a flow of comic business conceived at the height of Charlie's skill.

The millionaire gives Charlie his car and some money, and the next day Charlie is able to buy the flower-seller's complete stock. He drives her "home" in the car, but the millionaire, now cold sober, fails to recognize his new friend and takes back the car without a thought. However, drunk once more, he retrieves Charlie and gives a party in his honor. At the party, Charlie swallows a toy whistle. Sober again, the millionaire has Charlie thrown out. However, throughout these changes in his life, Charlie has to maintain the illusion of wealth with the girl, who becomes ill. He works as a street cleaner, but this overwhelms him when a procession of elephants passes by. He works as a boxer's stooge, and in the finest of Charlie's boxing sprees, faces yet another Goliath in the ring. He encounters the millionaire again, who is drunk enough to recognize him and give him the money needed for an operation to restore the blind girl's sight; but later he refuses to know him when he is accused of theft. Charlie manages to give the girl the money, but he is picked up and sent to prison. In any case, he dreads the girl's reaction to his appearance after her sight is restored.

It is autumn when he is eventually released. The girl is cured and waiting in her florist's shop, a sign of her good fortune, for the rich man who befriended her in the past to come back to her again. Destitute, Charlie wanders the streets in search of her. When he finds her, he gazes at her in longing, but she does not know him. She is merely amused at his dazed expression. She presses a flower and a coin into his hands, and only when she momentarily touches him does she realize who it is. This recognition scene is one of infinite pathos; they stand together, looking into each other's eyes. The scene fades in the atmosphere of ambiguity — her attempt to absorb the devastating truth, his dubious hope that she will ever now come back to him.

Charlie's approach to music composition for *City Lights* reveals another facet of his perfectionism. He could not read a note of music, working by ear only on his violin, the instrument he had played since his earliest times in the music hall, along with the cello. He also had a pipe-organ installed in his home on which he liked to improvise for hours on end. From *The Kid* onward, he had supervised carefully the cue sheets for the cinema music directions which went out with the films. These cue sheets could be complex, introducing recurrent character motifs, such as "La Violetera" for the flower girl in *City Lights,* and involved switching with the action from theme to theme (using passages from established music). But once Charlie had got a sound track at his disposal, he could not only compose the themes himself, he could control their orchestration and conduct the recording. In the process of transferring his ideas into practical musical notation, he destroyed the patience of the professional Hollywood composers and music directors he employed, Alfred Newman, David Raksin and Edward Powell. He used a recording instrument like a Dictaphone into which he hummed the effects he wanted, and working his helpers up to twenty hours a day forced them to try and try again to achieve exactly what he wanted, continuously changing everything until their nerves were shattered. According to Charles Chaplin, Jr., in his study of his father, Newman resigned before the score for *City Lights* was finished, while Powell would rush out in tears, strained to the breaking point by overwork and the ceaseless demands of his artistic persecutor. Theodore Huff states there are some ninety-five cues for changes in musical themes in the eighty-seven minutes of the film, threading together touches of established music with new themes in Charlie's characteristic style, drawing on various forms — waltzes, lively tunes, tangos, and strongly marked romantic phrases.

A second trip to Europe, as part of a world tour, and five years' absence from the screen separated *City Lights* from Charlie's next film, *Modern Times* (February 1936). *Modern Times* was to presage a new style, a new approach and attitude in Charlie's work. It moves in the direction of social comment, social satire. Technically, it remained in effect a silent film, except for the ironic gibberish Charlie sang at the end. But its conception derived from the increasing social conscience which Charlie had been developing from his wide reading, his discussions with men and women involved in politics and social studies, and from his travels and intuitive, emotional response to the society of his time — this was the period of the world depression, of industrial rehabilitation and expansion, and the era of Lenin, Stalin, and the Russian revolution, and of Hitler and the oppression of Europe. *Modern Times* was the first of Charlie's films, whatever his intentions, to lay itself open in certain sequences to wild, nonsensical charges of being "Leftist" propaganda.

In the meantime, Charlie had acquired a new leading lady and, later, wife in Paulette Goddard. She was more mature, more intelligent and, though ambitious, far more sympathetic and understanding than his previous child-wives had been. As we shall see, though their association from 1932 was an open one, their marriage was kept secret. Paulette was to remain with him until 1940, and star effectively in both *Modern Times* and *The Great Dictator*. Work on the first of these films began in October 1934. It was the first time that Charlie had written a full screenplay, and as a result of this more precise preparation he worked somewhat faster (ten months) and exposed less film (215,000 feet). The main vocal touches, apart from Charlie's gibberish song, were introduced as mechanical sound effects in the action — loudspeaker announcements and the like. The dialogue remained as printed captions.

According to the autobiography, Charlie was inspired by Paulette to create a gamine character for his film. He also had an idea to give some exposure to the factory-belt system, which could make nervous wrecks of some men — the tramp, working on the belt, has a nervous breakdown. So the tramp and the gamine, odd people out, pass through the malaise of modern times — unemployment, strikes, riots and so forth. The film opened with the title, "*Modern Times* is the story of industry, of individual enterprise — humanity crusading in the pursuit of happiness." Charlie refused to recognize in the film any of the left-wing propaganda his detractors insisted was implied. "There are those who always attach social significance to my work. It has none," he is quoted as saying.

"To entertain is my first consideration. . . . I have no political aims whatsoever as an actor," he has said. The film merely resulted, he claimed, from an impulse to say something about men becoming standardized, turned into machines.*

The film opens with Charlie on the belt, jostling fellow workers in his efforts to keep up with a dual nut-bolting operation. He is caught up in a large machine like a rolling mill, which sucks him in and for a while imprisons him in its gears and rollers. He is chosen as the worker on whom a new feeding machine (feed-while-you-work) is to be tested. The machine goes berserk, and Charlie's face and mouth are inundated with unwanted food. Back on the belt, he goes crazy, dancing with the two wrenches held out like antlers, and carrying on like Pan. He dashes into the street, tightening anything which looks to him like a nut. He encounters a stout lady with two large buttons on the bosom of her dress. He is seized and put in a mental clinic.

Once out of the hospital, he has to face unemployment. The moment he gets a job, the workers decide to come out on strike. He steals a lift on an explosives truck, but is thrown off its tailboard clutching its red danger flag. Immediately a flock of Communists rush to follow him. Back in prison, he prevents a jailbreak and is rewarded with a life of ease, broken only by the bad news that he is to be released.

Working in a shipyard, he unfortunately launches, and sinks, a new ship, and only his interest in a new acquaintance, the gamine, prevents him from commiting petty crimes in order to get himself arrested and live at ease in prison. He and the gamine set up home together in "Paradise," a hut by the waterside with a dog kennel in which Charlie

---

* In 1937 a plagiarism suit against Charlie was initiated by the producers of René Clair's film *A Nous la Liberté* (1931). Clair himself was against the suit, and it was finally dropped.

virtuously tries to sleep, leaving the hut for the lady. Working next as a night watchman in a large store, he admits the girl after dark so that she can sleep in one of the luxurious beds on display. He welcomes a group of unemployed men who are attempting to raid the store. So, to his relief, he is sent back to prison.

On his release once more, he and the girl work in a cabaret, she as a dancer, he as a waiter. There is an Essanay-like sequence with a roast duck which has been ordered by a guest. Charlie is finally forced to deputize for an absent singer, and muddling up the words hastily written on his cuff, comes out with the famous gibberish song in a pastiche of foreign languages. The welfare officer arrives to take charge of the girl as a vagrant, but the two of them make a successful escape together, and are finally seen walking arm-in-arm up the traditional road which leads out to the horizon.

Though highly entertaining, *Modern Times* had little social comment and no political party implications whatsoever. It made no headway in the Soviet Union, and was banned in both Germany and Italy. It was only moderately successful in the United States, but a great success in those countries in Europe which exhibited it.

As a result of ten years' work, from *The Gold Rush* to *Modern Times,* Charlie, now in his middle forties, was a multimillionaire. But the "little fella," as the world had come to know and love him, was finished, destroyed by the coming of sound and the intrusion of the human voice on the screen. Charlie, too, had lost his innocence in the eyes of the public. For many people, he was a suspect figure — suspect for his morals and overpublicized associations with women, suspect for the left-wing politics he was too readily assumed to have. The uneasy story of his private life and of his supposed beliefs became confused with his work as an artist during the 1930s. It is necessary, therefore, to see to what extent elements in his private life had been forced into the public gaze, creating a drama of their own, which both the press and many self-appointed critics chose to use against him.

FIVE

❧

Adulation and Acrimony

THE MOST DIFFICULT ASPECT of Charlie's career is the private life that he was forced to live in public. He is often quoted as saying, "Comedy is life viewed from a distance; tragedy, life in a close-up." Charlie's films have been, in one sense at least, Charlie himself viewed through the distancing mirror of his art; the private life, which he has for the greater part of the time anxiously attempted to keep from public scrutiny, has born many of the signs of tragedy, though tragedy freely mingled with the absurd. It is the public private, private public sector of his life which reveals most tellingly the dichotomy in Charlie's nature, and the dichotomy also within the period in which he has lived, and within the public who have both overidolized and overpersecuted him. The idolization sprang from the extraordinary speed of the worldwide recognition of his genius, which could only have been effected by the rapid, universal dissemination of his image through the cinema, still less than twenty years old when he entered it; the persecution arose with almost equal rapidity because the mass-circulation press (itself scarcely older than the cinema) was able to exploit wide-scale public interest in the scandals which came to be associated with his name.

But the dichotomy was deep in Charlie himself. At one and the same time, he exploited and resented his phenomenal fame. He both gloried in it and loathed the results of it. All this has to be understood as something quite new in the human scene. In 1913 the name of Charlie Chaplin was all but unknown, except within the narrow circles of his profession, and even there Mack Sennett could not remember it exactly. By the end of 1914 he was so universally known and acclaimed he could multiply his salary ten times over at the close of each year's work until he became by the 1920s a self-employed multimillionaire. This was a phenomenon of the popular cinema and the popular press, the mass circulation of the image of one man. Charlie no more understood it than the public themselves. It simply happened to him. He was naturally caught up in the endless excitement of it all, and found the sudden accretion of money a fabulous miracle.

What neither he nor anyone else could be expected to understand at the time was the price that had to be paid for this sudden fame. To begin with he was only interested in the improvements money brought to his standard of living. He was naturally, as the result of hard experience during the years of his poverty, a thrifty man — some said, without full understanding of him, thrifty to the point of meanness — but he liked very much what money could buy (witness his twenty-four hours at the Astor in New York in 1913). It was not until the close of 1914, when his success was assured through his work at Keystone, that he says he moved from the small Great Northern Hotel to a twelve-dollar-a-week room at the Los Angeles Athletic Club, where he claims he lived sumptuously for seventy-five dollars a week, even allowing for drinks and the occasional dinner for others. He occupied a large corner room, he says, on the top floor, with a piano and space for his growing library. It was at this time that he asked Sennett to renew his contract at $1,000 a week, which Sennett refused, only to lose Charlie to Essanay at $1,250 a week with a bonus of $10,000 on signature of the contract. "It was bewildering, frightening — but wonderful!" Charlie had said then. At about the same time, Sydney was signed by Keystone at $200 a week, which was about what Charlie himself had been earning with the small bonuses his films were bringing him.

In 1915, Sydney, in addition to his performances at Keystone, began to assume the role of Charlie's business manager. He helped to negotiate the phenomenal contract with Mutual in February 1916 which brought Charlie $10,000 a week with a bonus of $150,000. On the strength of this, Charlie says that he bought himself a dozen neckties. The extra money, now a fortune, went into the bank; at the age of twenty-six, Charlie was a world figure, and Sydney had been able to leave Keystone around January 1916 to become his brother's full-time manager, and occasional actor in his films. For a while, early in 1916, Charlie writes that he occupied a house in Santa Monica facing the sea, but his basic residence, apart from hotels, appears to have remained the Los Angeles Athletic Club until his first marriage in October 1918.

Charlie's journey to New York, which ended in the signing of the agreement with Mutual, gave him his first real taste of public admiration. He traveled on a slow train, leaving immediately after he had completed *Carmen*. The mayor of Amarillo, Texas, was out in force with his fellow citizens to greet the great comedian who, totally unnerved, was in the washroom shaving. When he emerged, he was mobbed by an excited crowd, and entertained with sandwiches and drinks.

Charlie returned to his compartment much shaken. People began to pass up and down the train to catch a sight of him. He says he could not "digest" what had happened, but sat "tense," at once "elated and depressed." Then all along the line of the journey people turned out to greet him — at Kansas City, where the station was crowded and he had to mount the roof of the coach; at Chicago, where a suite of rooms at the Blackstone Hotel was placed at his disposal. Before he reached New York, the Chief of Police sent a message asking him to leave the train at 125th Street, since Grand Central was threatened with overcrowding. Crowds had indeed been gathering since early morning.

The presence of these crowds only enhanced Charlie's feeling of isolation. All he felt he wanted was to see Hetty, who he knew was staying with her sister in New York. He spent his free time wandering unrecognized in the streets and standing like an adolescent lover outside the apartment block where he knew Hetty was, afraid to go in. Later (as we have seen) he stood in the crowd in Times Square reading the electric sign on the Times building: "Chaplin signs with Mutual at $670,000 a year."

Nat Goodwin, the American Shakespearean actor, once a friend of Henry Irving and now, in his retirement, a respected friend of Charlie, had warned him, in the face of his phenomenal success, to keep out of the public eye. The urge to go out, to be seen and admired, was fatal to the illusion which the great actor should foster. To mix in society is ultimately to destroy that illusion, he was warned. "You've captivated the world," said Goodwin, "and you can continue to do so if you stand outside it."

It was a dilemma he was not to resolve. He liked most to be alone, especially when pondering ideas for films. He liked long, solitary walks, in cities, in the countryside, or by the ocean. Yet the growing public adulation made his pulse race; he longed to tell people who he was and watch for their reaction. Then he would have liked to become the invisible man, spirited away to the comforts of solitariness

— to play music, to read, to go to bed, to do as he wished, and meet only the friends he wanted to meet at the times he chose. His vanity demanded it both ways. He was still flattered when the famous wanted to meet him, as they were beginning to do, such as the distinguished actor Sir Herbert Beerbohm Tree, in New York, and the great tenor Caruso. Often at such moments he was tongue-tied unless he could strike some chord of intimacy with these eminent strangers; then, warm and relieved, he would spill over with friendliness. But he was normally on the defensive; as he has said, "I like my friends as I like music — when I am in the mood." But this makes the conduct of friendship difficult alike for them and for him.

After the Mutual contract, he began to build a shell around himself. He bought an expensive car and hired a chauffeur and a male secretary. The first notable secretary and man-of-all-work was Tom Harrington, ascetic yet bohemian, an American of Irish descent. He was self-effacing, educated, and brought books unobtrusively to his employer's attention. He became the almost invisible *alter ego* whom Charlie required, at once protecting him from the world and supplying his every want, asked or unasked. It was he who acquired the celebrated Japanese aide, Toraichi Kono, who worked initially as chauffeur but was soon to acquire an ever-ascending position in the Chaplin household until, with Harrington's departure in the early 1920s, he became the majordomo in Charlie's private life until the 1930s. For eighteen years, from 1917 to 1934, he was both watchdog and troubleshooter in the Chaplin menage. He claimed to come from a wealthy family in Hiroshima and to have rebelled against the family tradition, breaking with his father and emigrating to the United States, where he was finally forced to earn his living. When he entered Charlie's service he was twenty-nine. He was married and had a son, but his family was kept well in the background. Kono was to become

Charlie's devoted slave, traveling with him wherever he went. He was to have a great deal to endure.

Charlie has said, "I do not believe sex is the most important element in the complexity of behaviour. Cold, hunger and the shame of poverty are more likely to affect one's psychology." Sex, he continued, "was not the all-absorbing interest in my life. I had creative interests which were just as all-absorbing." Nevertheless, he has not hidden from the world that his interest in beautiful girls was frequently obsessive, and on more than one occasion came near to wrecking his career. His position in this was extraordinarily parallel to that of H. G. Wells, both in his inability to conceal his private life, and in the persecution he endured at the hands of an angry and affronted public, who did not feel that the men whose work they admired so much and rewarded so highly should be permitted to flout the sexual conventions which they, the public, felt forced to observe. Charlie and H. G. Wells, who were to become close friends, must have felt much in common, and Charlie was to be well acquainted with Wells's work and ideas. Novels such as *Ann Veronica* and *The New Machiavelli,* which advocated freer relations between the sexes, had appeared before the war and had caused Wells much trouble.

Left to himself, Charlie would probably have contented himself for a considerable period of his life with a series of more or less deep involvements with attractive girls, relationships which would have terminated when each tired of the other, or more likely when he tired of them. He claims that his sex life went in cycles, "like everybody else's." "During work, women never interested me," he says in his autobiography, and (significantly) he quotes Wells: "There comes a moment in the day when you have written in your pages in the morning, attended to your correspondence in the afternoon, and have nothing further to do. Then comes that hour when you are bored; that's the time for sex." "It was only between pictures, when I had nothing to do, that I was vulnerable," Charlie adds. In a sense, both Wells and Charlie, for all their assumed sophistication, were innocents abroad in this matter. They saw a girl they liked, they overwhelmed her with sudden compliments and ardent attention, they made love to her, and then found they had saddled themselves with a demanding female who became less and less willing to put up with their egocentric moods and habits, and the relationship deteriorated from bickering to outright alienation. Neither man seemed to recognize until it was far too late that only a very exceptional woman would understand how it was that at certain times she simply would not be wanted and at others ardently desired. Above all, in Charlie's case, they would not understand his absolute need for frequent periods of isolation and the occasional stimulus of the company, and perhaps the love, of other women. Wells, after some trial and error, found himself just such an understanding wife when still young, and never ceased to love her in spite of his prolonged absences and frequent periods of unfaithfulness. Charlie, until his comparative old age, never did.

What seems to have stood in his way was the child image of Hetty. As he developed into maturity, with the complexity and self-questioning of a great artist whose work was all-absorbing and wholly self-created, he retained an adolescent desire for the love of very young girls. They represented solace, comfort, an ineffable feminine sweetness which is difficult to comprehend in the 1970s. The postwar jazz age was not yet born, and when it was Charlie, by that time well into his thirties, was not affected by it. The Pollyanna image popularized by Mary Pickford was a form of retarded feminine charm (often accompanied by astuteness in stimulating and exploiting older men) which had survived from the nineteenth century and the cult of the pretty, insipid, mindless girls suitable for the Victorian harem. Charlie may have found solace with the easier going, more open and less astute girls which the twentieth century was already producing (such as the beautiful girl with whom he had spent a "romantic week" when he was on tour in St. Paul in 1913), but his inner heart seemed anchored in the girlish charms recollected in the Hetty of 1908.

It must also be remembered that Charlie himself had since his adolescence been very attractive. His early photographs show him as a serious young man with a strong chin, full lips, a long nose, dark eyes, pronounced eyebrows, and dark, curly hair parted in the middle. His minute, agile figure (five feet, four inches in height and only a hundred thirty pounds in weight at this time) was always immaculately dressed. His image on-screen, especially when he developed pathos ("the poet . . . the dreamer"), and his "loneliness" off-screen, offered powerful stimulants to women, and with his enormous salary he soon became the most eligible bachelor in Hollyood. Moreover, the press was hungry to link his name with now this, now that woman to satisfy the vicarious cravings and curiosity of women fans all over the world who could only dream of their charmer.

As far as the actresses he engaged were concerned, he preferred always a girl whose performance he could mold rather than one whose style and appearance were already formed. There was more than a touch of the Svengali in his handling of his leading ladies — they were, in effect, projections of the ideal image in his heart rather than performers in their own right. The long line of his leading ladies is interesting to consider in this light: Edna Purviance (1915–1923), a partnership which took Charlie into his early thirties, was wholesomely youthful (nineteen in 1914) and serene to the point of being placid and even motherly; Georgia Hale (1924; replacing the unfortunate Lita Grey,

Mrs. Chaplin II) was harder and more spirited in *The Gold Rush;* the seventeen-year-old Merna Kennedy (1926) was a friend of Lita Grey, and gave a relatively colorless performance in the troubled production of *The Circus;* the radiant Virginia Cherrill, who had never acted before, was twenty-two and a divorcée at the time of *City Lights;* Paulette Goddard (twenty-five at the period of *Modern Times* and thirty at the period of *The Great Dictator*) was the only one of his leading ladies Charlie actually went so far as to marry, and this when he was in his middle forties. Marilyn Nash, another newcomer giving a pleasant, if amateur performance, was the independent, but still basically romantic young lady of *Monsieur Verdoux* (made when Charlie was in his late fifties). Claire Bloom and Dawn Addams were youthful unknowns when Charlie made *Limelight* (1952) and *A King in New York* (1957). Only in his last film, *A Countess from Hong Kong* (1967), has he broken with this principle, and used a well-known star, Sophia Loren. Of all the actresses he launched, only the later ones, Paulette Goddard, Dawn Addams and, more especially, Claire Bloom, developed effective careers independently of their work with Charlie.

The only ones among his leading ladies with whom he enjoyed a private relationship of importance were Edna Purviance and Paulette Goddard. Since they were both very much in the public eye, the relationships were kept as far as possible from the press; the place and the time of Charlie's marriage to Paulette Goddard were kept secret until long after it had taken place, when secrecy no longer had any point. Edna Purviance, who worked with Charlie far longer than any other of his leading actresses, was the daughter of a miner in Nevada, and had been a typist. She had come to seek her fortune in Hollywood. Charlie was introduced to her in San Francisco while searching for a leading lady; he found her beautiful and also well educated, but she was rather sad and reserved, and lacking (it seemed) in humor. However, he engaged her to appear in his Essanay films because, as he put it, "she would at least be decorative." Her beauty was of the blond, classic, even statuesque kind, and she had a full figure. She was soon deeply in love with Charlie, and he with her. She took an apartment near the Athletic Club, where Charlie continued to live, and where she dined with him most evenings. They became inseparable, and as an unpretentious, calm and agreeable blond she became a perfect foil for Charlie's dark coloring and temperamental humor. In effect, she mothered him, forming the perfect companion, since she was never ruffled by his behavior. On the screen he taught her to play the self for which he loved her, imperturbably beautiful and quietly responsive and sympathetic, a type of heroine soon to become old-fashioned after the war. Finally, in an effort to develop her as a dramatic actress and launch her on a new career elsewhere, he featured her out of character as the demimondaine in *A Woman of Paris,* but, as we have seen, it launched her leading man, Adolphe Menjou. By the mid-twenties she no longer suited the modern screen, and Charlie allowed her a life pension of $250 a week.

Charlie's own explanation of their relationship is that they were for a long period inseparable and certainly contemplated marriage. However, he says that he did not want to marry, and Edna for a while fell in with his mood. "I was uncertain of her, and for that matter uncertain of myself." Then, he claims, Edna set out to make him jealous with the handsome Thomas Meighan, star of Paramount, and showed jealousy herself by fainting and sending for him if she thought he was paying too much attention to somebody else. Perhaps she felt she had a right by then to marriage, and adopted filmlike devices to precipitate it. If so, she failed. Their last excursion together was a trip to Hawaii in September 1917, after he had completed his assignment for Mutual.

Then, in the summer of 1918, he met the sixteen-year-old film actress Mildred Harris* at a party given by Sam Goldwyn, and at her request Charlie drove her home. As he tells the story, he was not immediately taken with her, but she pursued him by telephone and her beauty enticed him to meet her again and entertain her. She had golden hair, large blue eyes, and a childlike air, and Charlie found himself infatuated. For Mildred he was no doubt the sweetest man she had ever known, younger looking than his twenty-nine years, and darkly handsome. He was, moreover, very rich and very famous. She had no opportunity to discover that he was also one of the most difficult, demanding and complex men in Hollywood, though his secretary (Harrington), his chauffeur (Kono), and most of the people at the studio could have told her. As for Edna Purviance, she continued to work loyally with Charlie, whatever her private feelings may have been.

When Mildred claimed to be pregnant a marriage was hastily arranged. Charlie acknowledges, with aftersight, he approached the marriage with a sinking heart, and Kono bore this out when talking to Charlie's early biographer, Garith von Ulm. Mildred had the ambitious mother customary for adolescent actresses in Hollywood at this time; she was a wardrobe mistress at the Thomas H. Ince studio. She was determined to see matters put right, even though she thought Mildred too young to marry. The marriage took place in secret on the evening of October 23, 1918, carefully engineered by Tom Harrington so that the press would know nothing until it was over. Charlie did his usual day's

---

* In the autobiography, Charlie says he met her in 1917, but this must be in error for 1918. She was born in 1901, but Charlie also states she "was not quite nineteen" at the time of the marriage in October 1918. Among the biographers who maintain Charlie's first meeting with Mildred Harris was in 1918 are R. J. Minney and Theodore Huff.

work at the studio before leaving for the registrar's office. The next day at the studio Edna quietly congratulated him. She had seen the announcement in the paper.

The first domestic home Charlie established was at 2000 De Mille Drive, Lachman Park, North Hollywood. It was described for the press by a friend of Mildred's as a "symphony in lavender and ivory, exquisite in every detail," but the lease was only for six months. The pregnancy proved unfounded after all, though in the summer of 1919 a malformed baby was born who died within three days and was buried with Mildred's inscription, "The Little Mouse." Mildred meanwhile had tried to involve Charlie in a dispute over her contract with Louis B. Mayer, which was increased (as a result of her marriage) to $50,000 a year for six films. Charlie had refused to become involved. Soon their work (Charlie was finishing *The Kid*) and the loss of their child led to virtual, and finally to actual, separation. Charlie moved back to the Athletic Club.

Mildred's idea had been to domesticate Charlie, making him over into a model husband and father. This was doomed to fail before it started, though he would certainly have loved his child had it survived. But Charlie had to learn that his private affairs, when they reached the stage of breakdown, became a public entertainment, fostered by the lawyers and enlarged by the press. Mildred began to give interviews, and her charges of cruelty and failure of maintenance voiced against her husband began to make unhappy headlines, reaching their climax in 1920. Charlie offered a settlement, pending divorce, of $100,000, which Mildred at first accepted, and then refused to take further. There was, as we have seen, a very real threat that Mildred and her lawyers could attach all his assets, including the master print of *The Kid,* in which Charlie had invested almost $500,000. This had led to the dramatic expedition to Salt Lake City with 400,000 feet of film in 500 separate reels. Once in Utah, they were clear of Californian law. First National, with whom Charlie was in dispute, was also trying to use Mildred's case to attach the film. The divorce was finally granted in November 1920, and Mildred received her $100,000 and a share of the communal property. She had a checkered career after this — she lost her star status after appearing in De Mille's *Fool's Paradise* (1921); she was bankrupt in 1922; she was twice remarried, in 1923 and 1936, and she ended her career in vaudeville. She died of pneumonia in 1944, aged only forty-one.

No doubt many people would be critical of Charlie's conduct, but it would appear he was tricked into the marriage, though only after indulgence in an ardent love affair with a girl still in adolescence. However, since he was working on both *Sunnyside* and *The Kid* during the brief period of the marriage, his absolute need for concentration and isolation were constantly frustrated by the frivolity of his child-wife's demands for personal attention and her incessant party-giving. He indulged in his long, solitary walks; his days and nights were spent away from home. He would stay away at mealtimes. Mildred had servants and her own car and chauffeur to look after her needs, but to make matters worse her mother was installed in the house. After the six months' lease on the house in Lachman Park was up, Charlie moved his unwanted household to 674 South Oxford Drive in Beverly Hills. He was seen around with other girls; in fact, each of them tried to make the other jealous through apparent unfaithfulness. Kono was pressed into service to look after Charlie and protect him; Kono claimed later that he was forced to act as a spy on Mildred back at the house. He was loyal, but disinterested. It was Kono who was dragged from his bed to drive Charlie and the half-cut reels of *The Kid* to Utah; when they arrived at Salt Lake City they looked like tramps and had to reveal their identity when telegraphing Harrington to send money.

Charlie had been forced to learn the hardest way what an ill-conceived marriage could be like. He had lost a large sum of money in buying off Mildred, and in lawyers' fees. He had sunk further money in *The Kid,* and at the same worrying time he had been forced to challenge the shady practice of First National. It was the first bitter lesson he had received since his rise to fame, and it undoubtedly hardened him as a man and as a contender in business.

This was not the only trouble Charlie's prominence had brought him. His country was at war, and technically he was of an age to enlist. When America herself entered the war in 1917 he began to receive letters of complaint and even threat over why a man in his position hadn't volunteered. He received the white feathers traditionally sent to cowards. The press was also caustic, launching a campaign against him inspired by his detractors. Actually, he was medically examined, but it was found he did not meet the Army's physical requirements; in any case, people more enlightened than the letter writers realized that his films were the greatest contribution he could make to the war effort. They were unique in their capacity to maintain morale. Before the United States declared war, Charlie assisted at Red Cross parties, during one of which some rich woman donated $20,000 in order to sit beside him at dinner. In 1918, he took part in the third Liberty Bond drive along with Douglas Fairbanks and Mary Pickford. In April he addressed great crowds from the steps of the Sub-Treasury building in Wall Street; in Washington he was received formally by President Wilson, and danced in public with Marie Dressler. All of which led delirious citizens to buy war bonds on the spot. When he toured the south, a former Secretary of the Treasury refused to appear on the platform with him on the grounds that he was a "vulgar movie actor." So they appeared separately, Charlie attracting a crowd estimated at forty thousand, while the politician drew four hundred. His campaign sold millions of dollars' worth of bonds. During the tour, which he did not complete owing to exhaustion, Charlie visited Army training camps which gave him material for *Shoulder Arms*. He made and donated a Liberty Bond trailer for the cinemas; in it he was seen married to Edna, the marriage bond shown alongside the Liberty Bond.

The theme of Charlie going to war became, in a manner akin to folklore, caught up in the popular songs of the day. The children in the streets had a play song, sung both in England and America:

> *One, two, three, four,*
> *Charlie Chaplin went to war,*
> *He taught the nurses how to dance,*
> *And this is what he taught them:*
> *Heel, toe, over we go.*
> *Heel, toe, over we go,*
> *Salute to the King*
> *And bow to the Queen*
> *And turn your back on the Kaiserin.*

In the trenches, the soldiers sang to the tune of the popular song "Red Wing":

> *For the moon shines bright on Charlie Chaplin*
> *His shoes are cracking*
> *For want of blacking*
> *And his little baggy trousers will want mendin'*
> *Before they send him*
> *To the Dardanelles.*

Charlie was also criticized for his treatment of his mother. After the war, Hannah Chaplin's health improved sufficiently for the brothers to be able to bring her to the United

States. Tom Harrington was sent to England to accompany Mrs. Chaplin on the voyage across; her mental condition made immigration difficult, especially when she addressed the immigration officer as Jesus Christ. She was admitted on the strict understanding that Charlie would take total responsibility for her, and she was given a house in Santa Monica and a staff to look after her. Charlie was criticized for everything imaginable — for not paying her fare, for not taking her into his own home. She had seen none of his films, and was quite incapable of understanding that he was a star and possessed great wealth. When he screened a film for her, she complained that they had made her beautiful son far too ugly. She remained in the greatest comfort in Hollywood until her death in 1930, but Charlie always found it deeply painful to visit her, or receive her in his house.

With the final achievement of his divorce, Charlie's name began to be linked with the names of other women, such as the actresses Claire Windsor and May Collins. It was sufficient for him to be seen out with them two or three times for rumors of an engagement to flourish. May Collins appeared in *The Shark Master,* and she was also an established stage actress; Claire Windsor, a tall, slender blond, was out to make a name. According to Theodore Huff, she plotted with a publicity man to be reported missing after going out on horseback into the hills. She was found, admitted to a hospital, and then Carl Robinson, Charlie's publicity director and stepson of William Fox, one of Hollywood's leading producers, found her sickly pallor was just makeup. The fact that Charlie had offered $1,000 reward for knowledge of her whereabouts was sufficient for the press, and helped her to achieve her ambition for stardom.

But Charlie's wayward relationships did not hide the fact that he was exhausted by the hard work of the past years. After the divorce, he had lived it up with parties in New

York. He had widened his circle of friends and acquaint-
ances — this now included Waldo Frank, Hart Crane, Max
Eastman, and Alexander Woollcott in New York, and Dr.
Cecil Reynolds, the English brain surgeon, who was living
in California, and with whom he loved catching tuna fish
off Catalina Island. It was not overlooked, of course, that
several of these friends were Leftists. He received letters
from H. G. Wells, and even one from Hetty, married, of
course, and living now in London. She invited him to come
and see her if he ever should return to England. So, with
the two-reeler, *The Idle Class,* completed, he ordered Carl
Robinson to get tickets for them both to leave for London.
He sent the company on vacation on the very eve of starting
Pay Day in August 1921. Syd's last instructions to Carl
Robinson were, "For God's sake, don't let him get married."

After giving a party in New York (at which he burlesqued
the death scene in *Camille,* dying himself instead of Camille
in the arms of Madame Maurice Maeterlinck, formerly the
actress Georgette Leblanc, after a comic coughing contest),
the magic trip began. Beforehand, however, he had to face
the press, with their barrage of foolish or impertinent ques-
tions such as, "What do you do with your old mustaches?"
"Do you expect to get married?" and "Are you a Bolshevik?"
To this last question he replied, "I am an artist. I am interested in life. Bolshevism is a new and challenging phase
of life. Therefore I must be interested in it." The rumors
proliferated — yes, he is a Bolshevist. Yes, he's going to
Russia — and so forth.

On board the *Olympic,* the ship which had brought him
back to the States, second class, in 1912, he soon found
there was a movie cameraman sent specially to cover his
activities. A news photographer tried to make him blow
kisses at the Statue of Liberty. He spent most of his time
with his friend Edward Knoblock, the English playwright,
who was also sailing, though he consented to go down to

the boiler room to play a game of cricket with the firemen and stokers. But every night he dined in black tie with Knoblock in the ship's most exclusive restaurant.

What Charlie had half hoped for was a restful, nostalgic homecoming, revisiting old haunts and seeing old friends. The dual response in his nature to acclamation, on the one hand, to being received like royalty, which excited his vanity ("I revel in it secretly," he confessed), and on the other hand to living as he wanted, in seclusion and privacy, was put to the test both in Cherbourg and London. As the ship touched Cherbourg, the French press poured on to interview "Charlot." They boarded the liner like pirates. He was seized with nerves, and gave answers which were only too easy to misunderstand; to the question whom he considered to be the greatest man, Lenin or Lloyd George, he replied that one works while the other plays. In Southampton, it was the same; the crush of reporters all but knocked him down. But he managed. There were friends here to greet him, including his cousin, the publican Aubrey Chaplin, and Hetty's brother, Sonny Kelly. He made his speech to the mayor of Southampton, and the side of him that welcomed adulation noticed that the crowds at Southampton were not so large as he had expected. After all, the press headlines had said "Homecoming of Comedian to Rival Armistice Day." Then on the train to London, Sonny Kelly leaned across and said in a strange, embarrassed voice, "Hetty died, you know."

Charlie says that he could not assimilate this. In a sense, he had come back only for her, with London as the nostalgic frame to the picture he carried of her in his memory. The English scene sped by the carriage windows, and they reached London. The train stopped at Waterloo station. The crowds here were of the size he had imagined they should be. But, Hetty was dead. He was seized by the station officials and rushed past the roped-off crowds into a limousine into which he plunged and found himself sitting beside his cousin, Aubrey. Charlie's eyes filled with tears as the car turned to cross Westminster Bridge with the Houses of Parliament on the skyline. Outside the Ritz Hotel, where he was staying, the throngs of people blocked the street. He was eventually forced to go out on a balcony and wave in response to their cheering. He told the press of friends inside the hotel that he must rest, but that he could meet them all at dinner. Then he changed his clothes and slipped out of the hotel through the back door.

He took a taxi to the Kennington Road. The place looked unchanged. He got out and walked around the block to find number 3 Pownall Terrace, where his mother had starved herself and lost her reason. It looked, he thought, like a gaunt old skull. He went on in the taxi to other places he had known, where he had lived or tried to live. At the entrance to Kennington Park he stopped and got out again. It was here that Hetty had come, jumping off the tramcar that Sunday morning. Now she was dead. He stopped at a familiar pub for a drink. But it all seemed unreal, smaller than life, drab and insignificant compared with Hollywood, the dream of the past compared with the reality of the present. "I felt as though I was viewing it under a glass," he wrote shortly afterward.

While in London, he is said to have received 73,000 letters within three days, nine of them from different women who claimed to be his mother, and some 700 from people who claimed to be related. Some were from old colleagues in the theater. A staff of secretaries had to be hired to sort the mail. He was invited to the Garrick Club, the club traditionally associated with the stage, where he met, among other distinguished men, the dramatist Sir James Barrie, who took him afterward to his apartment in the Adelphi overlooking the Thames for evening tea. Bernard Shaw also lived at the Adelphi, but they were not to meet on this occasion. However, he did meet H. G. Wells a number of times, spending an evening with him and Rebecca West, who was at that period living with Wells. While Charlie was in London, Wells screened for him a bad film adaptation of his novel *Mr. Kipps*. When meeting Wells, the most famous English novelist of the period, Charlie was at first nervous, but the conversation gradually warmed, and they talked about Russia, which Wells had just visited. Charlie discovered something of a kinship with Wells, and they were to meet again on his return to London.

Thomas Burke, whose *Limehouse Nights* had inspired Griffith's film *Broken Blossoms,* took him for a walk around London's Chinatown. Burke was later to describe Charlie as moody and dissatisfied with life:

> He is first and last an actor, possessed by this, that or the other. He lives only in a role, and without it he is lost. As he cannot find the inner Chaplin, there is nothing for him, at grievous moments, to retire into; he is compelled to merge himself, or be merged, in an imagined and super-imposed life. . . . This might explain some of the puzzling points about him. It might explain why he is unknowable. It might explain his unease and his dark charm. It might explain why he of all film actors has made a conquest of all the peoples of the world — because he is, like so many obscure millions, still the pilgrim; still looking for something and not knowing what it is. . . . Life seldom gives us just what we want; it gives us less or more. To most people recognized success comes only at the end of a weary plod. . . . Charles was given success, world-wide fame and a huge income in the best years of life, when they mean something — around twenty-five. He had no struggle for it, because he was never thinking of success in that measure. . . . It was no fine strength of character . . . that made Charlie successful. He was dowered with it. . . . All Charles did towards it was what his fellows around him were doing; he just went on working and doing his best. . . . [He has] that fierce vitality which is in itself a sign of genius.

He seems to spend his last ounce on whatever he is doing, and never at any time to have any reserves. . . . After a few hours with him, otherwise interesting and brilliant people seem unaccountably dull. Such cascades of talk! Such inexhaustible activity. Such exuberance of spirits — so long as there is company.

Charlie's comment on Burke is, "He drew me out. I felt I wanted to unburden my soul to him, and I did." He found Burke quiet, inscrutable, diffident, and looking like Keats. They had had similar backgrounds in their youth, and they took to each other.

Momentarily exhausted with London, Charlie had an impulse to go to Paris. Here he met through his friend Georges Carpentier, the boxer, the diplomat Sir Philip Sassoon. Sassoon was confidential secretary to Lloyd George, and was to become a close friend. He also met Anne Morgan, daughter of J. P. Morgan, who enticed him to appear at the premiere of *The Kid* in Paris which was to be put on in aid of funds for the rebuilding of devastated France, and she offered to recommend him for a decoration if he would only be present. Charlie could not resist this, and consented. Then he moved on to Berlin, where he was shocked to find he was quite unknown. *Shoulder Arms* had given offense, and had been banned after an initial showing; owing to the war his other films had scarcely reached Germany as yet. He had therefore no public reputation in Germany.

However, according to all accounts, Charlie was immediately smitten by the glamorous Polish film star, Pola Negri, who had made her name in Lubitsch's German films *Passion* and *Gypsy Blood*. She spoke no English, and he no German. Rumor had it that throughout his stay in Berlin, they were inseparable. However, this was hardly likely, since the actress was in the midst of an affair with a very demanding lover. Charlie in his autobiography makes light of this initial encounter, and says it lasted no more than "twenty minutes." But the acquaintance was sufficiently warm for Pola to count on it later when she came to Hollywood in 1923. Whatever may have happened between them in Berlin, much more was to happen in Hollywood. Pola Negri represented an altogether different kind of woman from those with whom Charlie had been familiar — she was exotic, sophisticated, dramatically passionate.

Before he left for the States, Charlie attended the premiere of *The Kid* at the Trocadero in Paris, receiving only a very minor decoration as reward — Officier de l'Instruction Publique. In England, he also spent a short time on Sir Philip Sassoon's estate. Sir Philip, Member of Parliament for Brighton and Hove, was one of the richest men in England and also one of the most altruistic in public life. A fruitful weekend was also spent with H. G. Wells and his family discussing politics. Charlie met as well St. John Ervine, the dramatist and critic, who shocked him by saying he was looking forward to the arrival of color cinematography and the talking film. Charlie maintained stoutly that the film was a pantomimic art and that speech would ruin it. It was even arranged for Charlie to meet Lloyd George, the Prime Minister, but an enterprising cinema manager "kidnapped" Charlie at the airport when he was returning from Paris, and rushed him to his theater in Clapham as a publicity stunt. Charlie took it in good part; it smacked of Sennett and Karno.

His last night in London he spent with his cousin Aubrey, visiting his public house in Bayswater. Back in the United States, and on the train to the West Coast, Charlie dictated his own, enthusiastic account of his visit to Europe, which was published as *My Trip Abroad*.

Charlie returned home elated, bemused, and of course lonely and depressed. He felt he had been transmuted into some kind of unique public phenomenon, and he was in little better position to account for it than an outside observer. He created his work by instinct, using the tools of his trade, and he brought a good and serious mind to bear on what he did, though without vitiating his intuitive judgment. He recognized that the cinema was a new, and universal star-making medium, and that through it, using wordless pantomime, the "little fella" he had created could reach the most distant places of the earth and receive recognition in all lands. He had had ample evidence on the Liberty Bond tours that others (Mary Pickford, for instance, and Douglas Fairbanks) had been able to draw vast crowds anxious to see in the flesh the people whose images they loved on the screen. But this only in part accounted for the phenomenon of his reception in England and France, the scale of it, and the joy it represented. Burke was no doubt right that at the base of it lay a strong element of identification; Charlie represented something most people wanted to have expressed about themselves, their resilience in adversity, their desire if not their ability to kick back when oppressed, their romantic sentiments. His pathos, his waiflike appeal and delicacy excited the sympathies of all women, while his agility and skill at inflicting a neat kick at his rivals and enemies delighted the men. Charlie embodied these human qualities, but above all he could make everyone laugh.

In time of war and universal suffering, the ability to create laughter is a gift beyond compare. Laughter in wartime is a healer, and laughter from the level of the Keystone knockabouts up to the imaginative humor of *Shoulder Arms* was the gift Charlie had given the world in over sixty films, or roughly one a month throughout the war years. It was a phenomenal record, bringing relief and release while at the same time appealing to so many humane values. Add to this, that everybody knew Charlie represented, to an

exceptional degree, the Cinderella story. From being phenomenally poor he had, as if by magic, become in a few years
phenomenally rich. He represented to the poorest among
his audiences a living example of the ability of man to conquer adversity and become a multimillionaire, appreciated
and courted even by the established rich, the titled, and the
heads of state, who presumably wanted to meet him as the
phenomenal artist rather than as the phenomenal success,
the parvenu. And since adulation breeds adulation, fed by
the popular press, the crowds turned out to see the little
man who was, they felt, more famous than anyone else in
the world, and yet had done nobody any harm.

Charlie's next brief but serious romantic association was
with the traveler and sculptress Clare Sheridan, a cousin of
Winston Churchill, and widow of a descendant of Sheridan
the dramatist. Her husband had been killed in the war. She
was the mother of a boy of six. At this particular time she
was a noted "free thinker" and pro-Bolshevik; she expressed
her views in a book, *From Mayfair to Moscow,* which was
tolerated as "eccentric" because of her impeccable social
connections. Much later, in the 1930s, she was to become a
Catholic. She had just returned from Russia, and was reputed to be the first Englishwoman to have penetrated the
headquarters of the Revolution. She had met Lenin and
Trotsky. On the other hand, she made busts of Atatürk and
Mussolini and, now she was in California on a lecture tour,
she did a bust of Charlie. Looking at it, he said in a remark
which became celebrated, "This could be the head of a
criminal." "No," she said, tongue-in-cheek, "it's the head of
a genius." Charlie at once claimed that the genius and the
criminal could be closely allied; both were supreme indi-
vidualists. It was May 1922, and they went off on holiday
together, taking the boy with them. Again, there were
rumors of a love affair. Clare wrote a discreet account of

it all, first in her *American Diary,* and later in her autobiography.

For Clare Sheridan, the meeting with Charlie appeared
a brief, imaginative, idyllic moment of intimate communication set within a life full of movement and contact with
interesting and eminent people. She found him "attractively
shy and diffident," but on the other hand she discovered it
to be "difficult to gauge to what extent he was natural or a
poseur." But without any doubt he was a "great artist." At
one moment he overflowed with genuine emotion, then "all
unexpectedly he would be straining for effect, looking out
upon life through the windows of an advertisement bureau."
On the whole, she felt, the real Charlie predominated over
the "sham Charlie," and the real amounted to "a very lov-
able personality." When the impulse took him, he behaved
like a spoiled child who had to have his way; everyone had
to jump to his bidding — like his sudden, all-sweeping decision to take Clare and her son Dick on a holiday. She
uses words like "elfin," "urchin" about him; he would dance
on the sands like Nijinsky, or "make impassioned speeches
to imaginary crowds." "Whatever he did, he did intensely,"
whether comic or tragic, she says.

Then in September 1922 Pola Negri arrived, determined
to recaptivate her friend of the previous year in Berlin. She
arrived to fulfill a contract with Paramount. Her marriage
to the Polish Count Dombski had just been dissolved, and
she had got rid of her importunate German lover. At
twenty-five, she was ready for fresh pastures, and for the
maximum in publicity she could achieve. Charlie was living
in a rented house in the Moorish style in Beachwood Drive,
Hollywood, prior to building in 1923 the house in Beverly
Hills which was to become his permanent home during the
remainder of his career in America, and it was here that he
entertained the tempestuous and uninhibited Polish star,

who was determined to make her mark both as Charlie's new fiancée and as an actress. It was an extraordinary situation which got out of control, "an exotic relationship" is Charlie's own description of it, adding sardonically that Paramount, which regarded the actress as a prime investment, was continually worried at the exhausted and overwrought state into which she worked herself over the marriage Charlie claims he never proposed in the first place.

In the midst of all this trouble, matters were made worse by the arrival of another exotic, a young society girl from Mexico who was determined to make her way in Hollywood by haunting Charlie's house and eventually penetrating his bedroom and going to bed in his pajamas. According to Kono, the affair ended in a free fight between the two women. True or not, the relationship with Pola finally exploded and disintegrated in ashes, and the press was left free to link Charlie's name with a succession of girls, including another exotic actress, Peggy Hopkins Joyce, who was at least good for suggesting certain ideas and characters useful to Charlie for *A Woman of Paris*.

Pola Negri's memoirs were published in the United States almost fifty years later, in 1970. Her account of the relationship differs radically from Charlie's. She claims she was not immediately smitten by him in Berlin, that she did not find him physically attractive, except for his hands, which he used most expressively, though they were never without a cigarette. She was still at the time with her German lover, Wolfgang George Schleber, who asked Charlie how the tramp character had developed, and received a discerning reply, "Herr Schleber, if I was as tall and handsome as you, there never would have been a tramp. You see, there would have been no need to hide." Charlie, she adds, never minded how self-revealing he was so long as he remained the focus of attention. When they met subsequently at lunch, he urged her, she says, to come to Hollywood. There is no implication she was seen continuously with Charlie in Berlin, rather that she was at the time preoccupied with Schleber and with the problem of her divorce from her Polish husband, which her mother bitterly opposed.

According to her, the association with Charlie began only around September 1922 in Hollywood. Her divorce had come through, but her love affair with Schleber was over and she felt lonely in a strange environment. She claims that Charlie threw himself at her. She accuses him of behaving badly, of living in a world of selfish fantasy, of having no sense of judgment or humor in his masochistic attitude to women. He serenaded her with a ten-piece Hawaiian band, he besieged her by telephone, he sent her flowers and presents. "I was told," she writes, "there could be no greater indication of the seriousness of his intentions, for he was notoriously miserly." When they discussed the problem of love, he said, "Love is a competition. There is always a victor and a victim." She claims that his ardor eventually prevailed over her loneliness.

Charlie seems to her to have been indulging in play-acting. It was, she says, as if part of him had never grown up as a result of his childhood experiences. He remained a child, but the childlike spontaneity which illuminated his art ceased in his private life. There he became spoiled and difficult; if crossed, he sulked; he would pick occasions for quarreling, though he also enjoyed apologizing afterward. He was often late for appointments, or simply did not turn up. Although absurdly jealous, he could be sweet, tender, loving, and his childlikeness excited the maternal instinct in women. She found him sympathetic over the problems that faced her when making her first film (*Bella Donna*, which she did not like) in the exacting and alien conditions of Hollywood. But soon she found both the love affair itself and the persistent attentions of the press a nervous distraction which began to affect her work. There was constant trouble between her and the studio, which eventually involved Charlie himself, who seemed to her to revel in the publicity their love affair was attracting. Finally, the relationship ended, but only, she feels, when Charlie had drained all the emotional play-acting out of it.

According to Sam Goldwyn, it was a much publicized photograph of Pola giving Charlie a kiss which started up the rumors of their association in Berlin; this was only a publicity stunt by an American impresario, Ben Blumenthal, who wanted Pola to make films in the States. Goldwyn, writing at the time of the height of the romance in Hollywood,* gives the impression that Pola was at least as pursuing as pursued. "I believe Miss Negri intends to marry Charlie," he writes in 1923, but adds, rather extraordinarily in the light of Pola Negri's version of the story, "Chaplin does not admit he is in love." However, he adds, "both are great artists, and therefore misunderstandings are bound to happen. . . . Domesticity does not fit into my conception of his character."

Goldywn, who came to know Charlie well during his earlier days in Hollywood, describes him as a "maze of contradictions," a man who "loves power." Money, he adds, contributes to this, making him both demand large sums and save the money he gets. He is a delightful companion, says Goldwyn, a great entertainer in private life, constantly improvising dances, caricatures and imitations, comic speeches. He mimed the key events in his European tour for Goldwyn on his return to the States. This capacity to improvise he takes over into his professional work, building it up afresh in the studio without using any script. On the other hand, in contrast to this intense activity, there are times when he will only sit silent, staring into space, refusing to communicate, or going on long walks by himself. His life, says Goldwyn, is "intensely personal, intensely

* In his book, *Behind the Screen,* published in 1923.

emotional," and he hates anything which interferes with his personal freedom. He agrees that his most notorious social failing is not turning up at parties and other social occasions to which he has been persuaded to accept invitations. He hates making or keeping appointments. Goldwyn believed this to be a psychological reaction to his years of impoverished bondage. Part of his attraction, especially for women, is "his quick and vivid response to the moment," his boyish excitement which breaks down any embarrassment when first meeting people he finds he likes, the intensity with which he listens to what others have to say, and the extraordinary quality he possesses which makes people feel sorry for him; a pathos possibly arising from "an enduring isolation." However intimate he may appear, adds Goldwyn, he is "a strange combination of emotionality and detachment," both isolated and watchful. "He is a poet — the great poet of the screen. . . . For Chaplin has brought from the borderland of the subconscious mind those emotions which he sets before you. In that single small figure . . . he reveals the loneliness and frailty, the lurking irresponsibility, the fears and aspirations — all the intermingled pathos and humor of the universal soul."

During the years 1922 and 1923, Charlie could be described as enjoying the company of women of the world, women who were sophisticated, experienced and, in some cases, like Clare Sheridan, of marked intelligence. But however absorbing they might be, they sapped his creative energies. His work in any case, as we have seen, had slowed down: between 1923 and 1930 he was to make only four features, *A Woman of Paris, The Gold Rush, The Circus,* and *City Lights,* the latter still basically a silent film. This was the troubled period of his second marriage, that to Lolita McMurry, which took place late in 1924.

However, just prior to this, Charlie's name became for a while closely linked with that of Marion Davies, who was universally recognized as the mistress of William Randolph Hearst. She had also developed into a brilliant and talented star of silent films, in spite of the overblown publicity accorded her in the Hearst press when she appeared in the succession of films Hearst promoted for her. She had been Hearst's mistress since 1915, when she was seventeen and he fifty-two; there was thirty-four years' difference in their ages. But Hearst was one of the most powerful — some said the most powerful — figures in the United States, and what he said was to happen normally happened, even to Marion, a former chorine and Ziegfeld Follies girl, whose independent spirit led her sometimes to be at war with her role as the most richly endowed mistress in the United States. She had had her differences with Hearst, and although she loved him she was not above showing her resentment by exciting his jealousy. Charlie, worried at the prospect of his second marriage, seemed to find her gay company indispensable, and they were often seen together during Hearst's frequent absences in New York. However, the scandal, if there was one, soon blew over. Charlie was subsequently to remain a friend of both Hearst and Marion, as his autobiography reveals. If there was any real jealousy on Hearst's part, it was (like so much else in Hearst's life) carefully hushed up.*

Lolita McMurry, whose mother, Lillian Grey Spicer, was Mexican, had appeared as an angel in *The Kid* at the age of twelve; both she and her mother had also appeared as maids in *The Idle Class*. In 1924, Charlie needed a new leading lady to replace Edna Purviance, who ranked now as

---

* Charlie was said to be one of the party on Hearst's yacht on the occasion of the well-known director Thomas H. Ince's mysterious heart attack, which led subsequently to his death. Fred Lawrence Guiles, biographer of Marion Davies, records there were suspicions Hearst had shot Ince in mistake for Charlie. There was no postmortem. After attending the funeral, Charlie left for Mexico where he married Lita Grey.

a "dramatic" actress and who was in any case looking far too "mature" at thirty for Charlie's needs in his new film, *The Gold Rush*. Lolita was sixteen, and was to use the professional name of Lita Grey; she was rather broad-featured, and her charm lay in her spirited manner. But she was, in fact, unintelligent and talentless, and at sixteen her education was technically incomplete. Strangely, when Charlie tested her she satisfied him, and he signed her in March 1924 at a salary of seventy-five dollars a week. He even began to take her around with him, and the press immediately sensed a "romance." Edna Purviance's dressing room was got ready for its new occupant, and the domineering Mrs. Spicer moved in as if to take charge of the studio. The publicity made young Lolita sound like some exotic fruit.

They rushed into marriage, he thirty-five, she sixteen. She was pregnant. To avoid the almost unavoidable, the press, Charlie pretended he was filming locations for *The Gold Rush* in Mexico; they were married on November 24, 1924 in Empalme, in the state of Sonora. Then they returned by train to Hollywood, with the press on their backs. Charlie kept to himself, while the McMurrys celebrated. They were to take over Charlie's new home in Beverly Hills. Not only Lita, but her mother and grandmother moved in, and the situation became intolerable. To satisfy the education authorities, Lita had to continue her formal education with hired tutors. When her pregnancy was announced, this was used as an excuse to withdraw her from *The Gold Rush;* her place was taken by Georgia Hale, and the sequences involving her were reshot.

On June 28, 1925, Lita gave birth to her first child, Charlie's first son, Charles Spencer Chaplin, Jr.* Some nine

---

* Charles Chaplin, Jr., in his book about his father, claims his mother told him he was actually born on May 5 — "The records were changed," she said. "He has all this power, you see." Considerable detail concerning this second marriage is given in such books as Carlyle T. Robinson's

months later, on March 30, 1926, a second son was born, Sydney Earle Chaplin. But the marriage was not, could never have been, successful. Lita was overyoung, extravagant, and liable to be difficult, especially with a husband over twice her age whom she was totally unfitted to understand. She took possession of Charlie's fine new mansion, and one night he returned from work on *The Circus,* on which he began work in 1926, to find a drunken party in progress. He became enraged. He cleared everyone out of the house, and the press of December 2, 1926, announced that husband and wife had formally separated, and that Lita had gone to live with her grandparents, taking her two babies with her.

Unhappily, with her uncle, the lawyer Edwin McMurry, acting as her attorney, Lita Chaplin filed a suit for divorce in January 1927 with a forty-two-page document of complaint which extended sensationally from "cruel and inhuman treatment" and infidelity to every sin she, or her legal advisers, cared to devise. As a result, an order restrained Charlie, or any of his associates (the studio, Kono, Reeves, United Artists, and so forth), from withdrawal of funds, or his assets in terms of film, from the state of California. Charlie, distraught, stopped work on the ill-fated film, *The Circus,* and had to endure a further problem because the government also alleged he owed $1,133,000 in unpaid tax. Meanwhile, the gutter press had a feast as a result of Lita's recurrent, overpublicized complaints, to which she added fuel by asserting she could name no fewer than five prominent film stars as his mistresses. She even made insinuations against Edna Purviance, on the grounds of her weekly allowance of $250, and against Merna Kennedy, the friend whom she herself had persuaded Charlie to star as

---

La Vérité sur Charlie Chaplin; Pierre Leprohon's *Charles Chaplin* (with substantial quotations from Robinson's book), and the books already cited by Garith von Ulm and Theodore Huff.

his leading lady in *The Circus.* The text of her petition was hawked around in the streets as a broadsheet selling at twenty-five cents a copy.

Charlie defended himself and his friendships as best he could. But the puritan belt in America made a meal of the situation, calling for the barring of all his films. Some states responded. Charlie was forced to stop work on *The Circus.* Beset on all sides he fled to New York, where he suffered a nervous collapse, and was for a period confined to his bed. He feared his career was at an end, and that what remained of his fortune would be forfeit. It is significant that no mention whatsoever of this marriage and its collapse appears in the pages of his otherwise very frank autobiography. The memory of it is, as it were, expunged from his life.

It was unfortunate that this scandal followed hard upon those involving Fatty Arbuckle, who had been forced to retire in 1921 following involvement in a horrifying fatality due to sexual excesses, and Mabel Normand, who had been involved in the Taylor murder case in 1922. In both instances, these artists' films were banned from the screen by the concerted action of the all-powerful women's clubs. H. L. Mencken wrote in the *Baltimore Sun,* "A public trial involving sexual accusations is made a carnival everywhere in the United States." Organized protests about the unfair treatment being given to Charlie came from France, supported by such prominent people as Germaine Dulac, the leading woman director, Louis Aragon, and René Clair. But Charlie was finally forced to come to a cash settlement, and the divorce was granted on August 22, 1927. The cost in all was in the region of a million dollars (including a trust fund for the children), and Lita kept custody of their two sons. She was subsequently to marry twice and divorce twice. Charlie had the resources to weather his losses in back tax and alimony, and before the Wall Street crash

occurred in 1929 he instinctively foresaw what was coming
and sold his stock in advance, keeping his money in fluid
capital.

Charlie maintained his social round, meeting personalities such as Albert Einstein, who was to become a friend,
Gertrude Stein, Elinor Glyn, and the European aristoc-
racy and crowned heads who assembled at the Fairbankses'
mansion near his house. Through the Fairbankses he had
originally met Marion Davies, and it was at the Georgian-
style beach house Hearst had given her at Santa Monica
that Charlie had several enjoyable meetings with Winston
Churchill, who was an enthusiastic admirer of his work.
His well-established friendships with Upton Sinclair, Max
Eastman and H. G. Wells, friendships which helped to
give him the reputation of being a Leftist, increased his
interest in social and political affairs. So did his many meetings with Lady Astor. In his autobiography he records
something of his arguments about socialism with Wells,
with whom he was to have frequent discussions. "Wells
wanted to know how I became interested in socialism. It
was not until I came to the United States and met Upton
Sinclair, I told him." As a result of his conversations with
Sinclair he "saw politics not as history but as an economic
problem." Wells had appealed to him very much as a man
with a background similar to his own: "Wells's humble
origin had left its mark, not in his work or outlook, but as
in my case, in an over-emphasis of personal sensitiveness.
I remember once he aspired an 'h' in the wrong place
and blushed to the roots of his hair. Such a little thing for
a great man to blush about."

Charlie's view of society had been arrived at intuitively,
as a result of experience, not academic or political training.
He had read widely by now as taste directed; he had met
interesting people, persuasive like Sinclair and Wells, from

whom he had derived, at least in part, the views which so much offended newsmen, clubmen and clubwomen when he, with a naïve sincerity, fired them off, sometimes with a desire to shock during the interviews which he so much disliked. "I cannot vociferate about national pride. . . . The fact is I am no patriot — not for moral or intellectual reasons alone, but because I have no feeling for it," as he says in the autobiography. He associated with people of all political persuasions simply because he liked them. He invited trouble because he could not keep his mouth shut, was often overtrusting in what he said to strangers (who were sometimes newsmen disguised as innocent citizens), and did not like practicing tact and diplomacy, which he felt was small-minded.

Anthony Asquith, the filmmaker son of a former British Prime Minister, met Charlie in Hollywood in the late 1920s and was struck not only by his infectious smile but by his love of theorizing:

Charlie's smile was essentially a smile of the eyes which did not necessarily need confirmation from his lips at all. It was largely the sense of immediate personal contact which his smile gave me and partly, no doubt, the dreamlike unreality of the setting that took away all shyness from me. I found myself talking to him as if I had known him for years.

Charlie was a great talker in every sense of the word and his conversation in those days, at any rate . . . was a curious mixture. He loved theorizing about Art and Life, Religion and Politics, and, though what he said was always interesting, it was not unlike the conversation of a clever undergraduate. It was the kind of conversation I had been accustomed to at various literary or philosophical societies at Oxford, but, when he left Life in the abstract, and came to living people, it was a very different thing. I have never known anyone to compare with him in the power to make real and vivid a person he had met or an incident he had seen in the street. It was not a question of mimicry or verbal description, it was an act of creation. He, himself, disappeared, leaving a kind of ectoplasm from which the people, the setting, the event, materialized.

His attitude to money is also intuitive. When the large sums came his way, he says he could never take them for granted. It was like an incredible windfall for a man still basically poor. He could not, he says, actually see the money. The only proof of its existence was to be able to go out and buy expensive things — clothes, cars, suites on trains and ships and at hotels, food and drink at top restaurants. These he tried to savor as long as possible: "The saddest thing I can imagine is to get used to luxury. Each day I stepped into the Carlton was like entering a golden paradise." Naturally, the Chaplin legend has represented him as both mean and generous, but like many very rich men who have known poverty, he is temperamental in his attitude to money, generous often with the "unseen" money represented by checks (he has helped innumerable people in his time for whom he has some sentimental regard), then suddenly careful when he suspects (rightly or wrongly) some advantage is being taken of him, as he can feel hard, tangible cash leaving his pocket. When he gives money away, he does so only as he wants, not as outsiders often think he should. Money, he has always realized, is something he has had to earn. His greatest dread has always been poverty, a return to the degradation and humiliation of his youth.

The great Russian director Sergei Eisenstein visited Hollywood in the summer of 1930. Eisenstein, aged thirty-two, was a volatile, mercurial man with a widely intellectual and inquiring mind about the arts and sciences. He had an enormous, boyish sense of fun, and a deep interest in the circus, clowning and pantomime. He was also interested in languages, and spoke French, German, Spanish, as well as

English. He had been for a long time an admirer of
Charlie's lyrical, acrobatic pantomime. Charlie, on the other
hand, was equally interested to meet the man who had
made the Soviet classics *The Battleship Potemkin* and
October. Indeed, Douglas Fairbanks, who had visited the
U.S.S.R. in 1926, had been instrumental in getting *Potemkin*
shown in the United States. Eisenstein, during a period of
leave granted him by the Soviet government, had received
an invitation from Paramount to visit Hollywood, bringing
with him his two associates, his assistant director Grigori
Alexandrov and his cameraman Eduard Tisse; Paramount
had offered him nine hundred dollars a week, a fortune in
his eyes, to prepare a script on an American subject.
Charlie's house became a kind of refuge from the strange,
bewildering, artificial world of Hollywood, with its naïve
reactions to the Soviet Union. Eisenstein found Charlie
unaccountably serious. Charlie himself speaks briefly but
admiringly of Eisenstein's films, especially the later *Ivan
the Terrible,* for its poetic treatment of history.

Eisenstein became the object of attack by right-wing and
anti-Semitic forces in the United States, and his contract
with Paramount collapsed in October. But he, his associates,
and the Russian-speaking Ivor Montagu from England,
who had accompanied him as friend, fellow philosopher
and interpreter and had worked with him on the film
scripts of *Sutter's Gold* and Dreiser's *An American Tragedy,*
remained for a while in Hollywood. Eisenstein finally went
with his Russian colleagues to Mexico in December to make
the ill-fated film *Que Viva Mexico!* with backing from
Upton Sinclair.

During the six months or so Eisenstein was in California
he was a constant guest at Charlie's home; Ivor Montagu
had carried letters of introduction from H. G. Wells and
Bernard Shaw, and the house in Beverly Hills became a
"second home." They were forever playing tennis on

Charlie's court, which was floodlit for play at night. They bathed in his swimming pool, which was designed in the shape of the bowler hat he wore on the screen. Montagu also mentions a party at which Luis Buñuel, newly arrived in Hollywood from Europe, entertained Charlie's two children, who were visiting their father, by pantomiming a matador, and teaching them to make passes with a pocket handkerchief. On Thanksgiving Day, Charlie, mellow and happy, reenacted for them the whole of *City Lights,* on which he was still working. Charlie, Montagu noticed, always identified himself with the director, not with the character he plays, who remained a third person, a character to be created. Later, he showed Montagu rough cuts of the film. He took them all on his yacht to Catalina Island, some twenty-two miles off the Pacific coast, canceling work at the studio for three days on the grounds that "he had not an idea in his head." Georgia Hale was also a constant guest and, says Montagu, seemed sincerely in love with Charlie. Nevertheless, Charlie told them in Georgia's presence that "a gypsy in San Francisco had warned him he would have three unhappy marriages before happiness. That was why, after his two divorces, he must not think of a third wedding."

Montagu also comments on Charlie's considerable library, and denies as false the common allegation in Hollywood that he was "money-mad." Rather, he valued his millions in the bank because without them he would have to forfeit his artistic independence as a filmmaker. For this he needed at least two million dollars capital. This lay behind his refusal to let his films be released in the Soviet Union. He had been offered for distribution throughout the whole U.S.S.R. an amount equal only to the takings of a single middle-sized city in America. Montagu describes Charlie as a combination of "toughness and sensitivity," with alternating "moods of pride and self-doubt." Writing as a Jew himself with a strong consciousness of race, Montagu adds:

> Charlie is not a Jew or of Jewish origin. He attributes his
> black curly hair in youth to a Spanish strain. But he has rig-
> orously refused ever to deny publicly that he is a Jew. He
> says that anyone who denies this in respect to himself plays
> into the hands of the anti-Semites. From Germany in the
> thirties I sent him the filthy Nazi propaganda book of photo-
> graphic portraits of Jews, *Juden sehen dich an*. His portrait
> was included and the caption began . . . "This little Jewish
> tumbler, as disgusting as he is boring . . ." . . . I like to think
> it had some part in stimulating *The Great Dictator*.

After finishing *City Lights,* which against all prognostica-
tion was a great success in New York, Charlie decided to go
to London for the premiere. It was the spring of 1931, and
the social round began again, largely primed by Sassoon
and Lady Astor, formerly an American from Virginia and
now a member of the British Parliament. Charlie met Lloyd
George and Bernard Shaw, both of whom he had missed
ten years before; Ramsay MacDonald (the Prime Minister),
H. G. Wells once again, and Winston Churchill, with
whom he spent a week at his country house, Chartwell.
Shaw sat beside him at the premiere of *City Lights,* while
Churchill made a gracious speech at the supper party afterward. Churchill at this time was out of office. Charlie even
met Gandhi, who was in London and living in a slum district off the East India Dock Road. On this occasion, as on
others, there were crowds around and the press stood at the
ready. Charlie declared that he sympathized with India's
desire for independence. In contrast, Charlie met the Prince
of Wales and was entertained by the Duke and Duchess of
York, and then accompanied the Duchess's brother, a boy
of thirteen, to Eton, where he was shown around England's
most famous school.

The visit to England was not without its frictions. He

was criticized for failing to fulfill a promise to visit the children at his old school in Hanwell, and for neglecting to answer an invitation to appear in the Royal Command Performance (a sacrosanct obligation), and he was tricked by a newspaperman (who did not reveal his calling) into declaring that he regarded patriotism in the form of killing people in war as something he could never respect. "Charlie Chaplin No Patriot" made banner headlines. Later, in the south of France where his brother Sydney was living in retirement, he met the biographer Emil Ludwig. In Vienna he had (he says) a brief, romantic love affair, and in Nice another, more prolonged, with May Reeves, who subsequently wrote a book about him in French, *Charlie Chaplin intime.* In Venice he felt melancholy, while in Paris he met King Albert of the Belgians at the Belgian Embassy and had lunch with the French premier, Aristide Briand, who invested him with the order of Chevalier of the Legion of Honor. In Marseilles he had an amusing encounter with the evangelist, Aimee Semple McPherson, who took to him in spite of her religious conscience. In Germany he almost dined with the aged President von Hindenburg — an engagement which had to be canceled on account of the old man's illness — and he was attacked by the pro-Nazi press. He left Germany, however, satisfied by the warmth of his reception, a contrast with his previous visit.

The world tour, lasting in all eight months, finally took Charlie, Sydney and Kono to Japan, where he was delighted to see the formal, traditional performances of Kabuki drama. He was with the son of the Prime Minister, Tsuyoki Inukai, when the latter was assassinated. He returned to the United States very depressed, wondering, indeed, whether he should retire, going to live in Hong Kong. However, America, in the grip of the Depression, was about to respond to President Roosevelt's New Deal policy. *City Lights* was doing well, and the money was coming in.

Charles Chaplin, Jr., has characterized his father at this period in the 1930s with considerable sympathy in his published study of him. He speaks of Charlie's need for privacy alike from the outside world and from his family, an element in him his two first wives never understood. "I am not so sure I should ever marry," Charles quotes him as saying. "When I work I am oblivious of the world, and it's difficult to ask any woman to be happy when at times I forget her very existence." He was a man of "strange and sombre depths." Yet he loved his two boys, welcomed them, wanted them.

He has an intense feeling for people, for them or against them, but he can express a sudden enthusiasm for someone, man or woman, stirring them to respond, and then as quickly lose interest, and drop them. He has an intense love for his properties, his homes, first in Hollywood, and later in Switzerland. The house in Beverly Hills was set in a hillside estate of some six acres, on which trees (firs, cedars, spruce, pine) had been planted to make a pathed woodland, a tennis court laid out and a swimming pool constructed. Charlie was a good tennis player and swimmer. The house itself was spacious, and initially had two floors; there was a large entrance hall, running the length of the house, with a balcony at one end to which the staircase mounted. Charlie's pipe organ stood in a spacious vestibule off this hall, the pipes reaching up to the floor above. The vestibule also served as a projection theater for films, the screen dropping down in front of the organ. The living room was elegant, with large windows overlooking the terraced lawn behind the house. It had a fireplace in the English style, flanked by large bookcases. The living room housed a Steinway grand piano and a large Japanese cabinet full of sou-

venirs from Japan. Later, a study was added as a further
retreat for Charlie. The dining room with its massive dining
table also opened onto the lawn. The bedrooms upstairs all
had individual bathrooms, Charlie's bathroom smelling
strongly of his favourite Mitsouko cologne.

Charlie had a profound sense of ownership in relation to
this house, which by top Hollywood standards remained of
moderate size. His sense of privacy made him insist on the
boys knocking on doors before they entered. He exacted
good manners, courtesy at table, opening doors for ladies,
and so forth. The food served was very English and had
little variety; it was plain, home cooking. Tea and crumpets
were a specialty at four o'clock in the afternoon. Charlie's
house servants were Japanese; his gardener, a Mexican. He
liked the perfectionism of the Japanese, to whom (though he
remained absolute master) he left the running of the house.
When Kono left, he was succeeded by Frank, another
Japanese, as head servant.

When Charlie worked, everyone observed his need for
uninterrupted concentration, culminating in the actual making of the films. The family was sacrificed ruthlessly. "Everyone associated with him during these periods, either in the
studio or at home, was drained." He worked for prolonged
periods on his scripts — more than two years, says Charles,
on *Modern Times,* beginning immediately on his return
from his tour overseas. He loved the act of writing, but
hated any interruption while doing so. There he sat, head
bent, glasses on nose, a "tender, absorbed expression on his
face." When he was happy, he would sing; when he was
depressed, he would keep quiet. The moody spells were
oppressive, familiar to everyone who was close to him. Re-
laxation meant a game of tennis, a real release, something
which others might find in alcohol.

In spite of his care over money, he kept his devoted em-

ployees on the payroll when the studio was closed. However, he was just as much a perfectionist over saving money
and cutting costs as he was over his art. He would drive his
executive staff into the wall with his demands. His business
manager, Alf Reeves, took the weight of this, working with
Charlie from 1918 to 1946, the year he died. Reeves became
a vice-president of the Chaplin Film Corporation. Charlie's
radical, nonconformist views and his political reputation,
so largely false, were complemented by a highly conservative, not to say "capitalistic," outlook about his standard of
living. His clothes were always neat and conventional, like
his distinguished appearance, with graying hair early in life.
Charlie enjoyed everything traditional, especially humor,
and English customs, like the family Christmas, when he
had a family with him to enjoy it. But the autocrat was
never far distant from Charlie's nature.

The autocrat was most apparent when he was directing
his fellow performers, the insistence on detail, on constant
repetition, wearing down the vitality of those unused to
such an absolute approach to perfectionism. He himself
would arrive home exhausted from the studio, be helped
upstairs by his sons, and would flop down on his bed. After
a film was completed he would take to his bed for a day or
two to recuperate. Yet once recovered, and in a social mood,
no one could throw more energy into being a good host at
a party. His parties for the friends he really liked became
famous for the entertainment he gave them as a performer.
Many who visited him have described these performances.
He would dance and mime for his guests in one-man shows;
he would mimic opera singers, using pastiche languages.
He could even make Greta Garbo laugh. He could burlesque German, French, or Italian. He also loved to mime
improvised scenes from silent movies, snatching some girl
from among his guests to act as a foil, and playing in perfect

slow motion. These parlor games were often repeated, Charlie aiming at perfection even as a home entertainer.

In spite of the gypsy fortune-teller, Charlie was to enter on a third marriage during the 1930s. This was with Paulette Goddard, whom he first met on Joseph Schenck's yacht when she was an "extra"— a dancer and chorus girl with minor experience in a number of films and stage shows. She had been married in 1927 to a wealthy playboy, but divorced in 1931, when she was still only twenty. She was very intelligent and very ambitious, and when Charlie met her in 1932 she was a vivacious blond. He put her under contract, persuaded her to allow her hair to return to its natural, brown coloring, and put her into training for voice production and dancing prior to making her his leading lady, the gamine in *Modern Times,* on which work was finally begun in October 1934, lasting ten months. Charlie says their immediate response to each other was due to their mutual loneliness; he bought a boat on which they spent weekends off Catalina Island. They associated together openly, and after the release of *Modern Times* in 1936, they were married during a five-month trip to Honolulu, Hong Kong and Japan. But although Paulette Goddard was a mature woman and a genuine actress, she proved in the end unequal to the task of maintaining marriage with Charlie, though she understood his needs for solitude and concentration when working or preparing to work, and was good to the boys when they visited their father. The marriage itself, for some unexplained reason, was for long kept secret, although Paulette was living in Charlie's house and running it with such a display of domestic efficiency that Kono, after years in Charlie's service, felt forced to retire in 1934. Her long association with Charlie lasted until their divorce in 1940. After *Modern Times,* she had gone on to star in other films in her own right, though her resolute refusal to say whether or not she was actually married to Charlie apparently lost her a possible opportunity to be cast as Scarlet O'Hara in *Gone with the Wind*. The American women's clubs would not stand for such defiantly unconventional behavior. Their final parting in 1940, although according to Charlie inevitable, was nevertheless a "wrench."

Once again, this time at the age of fifty-one, Charlie was alone.

SIX

The Path to Exile
1940-1952

THE IDEA for *The Great Dictator* came originally from Alexander Korda as early as 1937. The resemblance between Charlie and Hitler, which stopped short at the mustache, had been the subject of amused comment throughout the 1930s, and Charlie's films were in any case banned in Nazi Germany. Korda had suggested a comedy based on mistaken identity, and as Charlie turned the idea over in his mind he realized, he has said, how his greatest problem in the sound film, letting the "little fella" talk, could be overcome yet again — as a burlesque Hitler he could extend his facility for playing with foreign-language jargon, as he had in the waiter's song at the end of *Modern Times*, while as the "little fella" himself he could restrict speech to a minimum and resort, as always, to pantomime. Charlie prepared himself to write the script during 1938, and completed it during the first six months of 1939. The first phases of production, tests and so forth, began in June, when everyone in the United States was anxiously waiting to see whether or not war would break out in Europe. Hitler had already taken over Czechoslovakia, and seemed poised on the brink of invading Poland. The British and French gov-

ernments had abandoned appeasement, and seemed ready
to stand by their commitments.

Charlie's position was not easy. So long as there were
German diplomatic representatives in Washington, strong
pressures could be brought to bear against any film which
either directly or indirectly "insulted" the head of the German state. This meant that, with the honorable exception
of the American screen magazine series *The March of Time,*
the American cinema, in common with the British and
French, had avoided any form of dramatization exposing
the nature of the Nazi regime. As Hitler's aggressive policy
came increasingly into the open, American anti-Nazi feeling found expression in a documentary-type melodrama
about Nazi activity in the United States itself — Anatole
Litvak's *Confessions of a Nazi Spy,* which appeared in the
spring of 1939. Among the very few films of 1940 dealing
with the situation in Europe (unfortunately, mainly in
terms of melodrama), the best was undoubtedly Frank
Borzage's *The Mortal Storm* (derived from a celebrated
novel by Phyllis Bottome), though Hitchcock's *Foreign
Correspondent* (August 1940) brilliantly exploited the ten-
sions in Europe just prior to the outbreak of war.

Charlie was working, therefore, entirely out on a limb
throughout 1939 in preparing to make *The Great Dictator.*
Indeed, he halted advance work in production for a few
days on the outbreak of war itself, but resumed it on
September 9 when he decided that ridicule was after all as
good a way to expose the pretensions of Hitler as serious
drama. It was to be his most expensive project so far, costing over two million dollars of his own money, and shooting
alone lasted until March 1940. He was under pressure from
United Artists to abandon the film; censorship was feared,
since the United States was not at war with Germany.
Charlie began to receive threatening letters from Nazi sym-
pathizers. But whatever the warnings, he was determined to

go ahead with a film which, as he put it, ridicules the Nazis' "mystic bilge about a pure-blooded race." However, writing with hindsight, he adds, "Had I known of the actual horrors of the German concentration camps, I would not have made *The Great Dictator*. I could not have made fun of the homicidal insanity of the Nazis."

The film began with a title: "Any resemblance between Hynkel the dictator and the Jewish barber is purely coincidental." Charlie is, of course, both at once — no longer the tramp, but a much tidied-up "little fella," spruce in a barber's white jacket or neat and agile in his dictator's uniform. The film is set primarily in the between-war period, but there is also a prologue showing Charlie as the Tomanian barber-conscript doing his best to make the huge, long-distance-range German gun of the First World War known as Big Bertha erase Notre Dame, which is seventy-five miles away, and ridiculing the situation in the style of *Shoulder Arms.* When he speaks, it is with a barber's careful politeness — "Pardon me, sir . . ." He suffers amnesia, but this carries him forward into the period when Adenoid Hynkel has already seized power in Tomania. Hynkel is introduced in a brilliant takeoff of Hitler at a high-power rally addressing the assembled multitudes in multilingual gibberish ("Democratia shtunk! Libertad shtunk!") which is freely translated over the radio into polite English ("Liberty is odious," and so forth). The applause switches on and off at a gesture from the Leader; the microphones bend back before his rage at the very thought of the Jews. There is comic business with his senior ministers, Herring and Garbitsch, before the Leader's departure, and sinister reference to the ghetto.

In the ghetto, where marching storm troopers mock the Jews, the little barber goes back to his unused shop from the hospital. He is still suffering from the effects of his amnesia, and he does not understand when the word "Jew"

is painted on the window outside his shop. He has trouble
with the storm troopers, but in his innocence, he answers
them back and is beaten for his pains, while Hannah, the
spirited Jewish gamine, bangs them on the head with a
frying pan one-by-one, when she can reach them from her
place of concealment. He is rescued by Schultz, a high-
ranking Nazi officer, because he once saved Schultz's life
during the war.

While Hynkel parades his power in his palace, the barber,
being so forgetful of his trade, tries to shave Hannah.
Garbitsch feeds Hynkel's vanity with dreams of world conquest and a civilization founded on a blond and pure-
blooded "Aryan" race. This is followed by the wonderful
sequence in which Hynkel dances with the huge balloon
globe — a curious mixture of gracefulness and paranoia.
The balloon finally bursts, and Hynkel breaks into sobs,
his dream vanished. The music used is the Prelude to
Wagner's *Lohengrin*. In an interview, Charlie said it was
like "merging Napoleon with Nijinsky." He is quoted by
Huff as saying, "All my repressed desires are fulfilled in
writing, directing and playing such a picture. With the
dictator and myself, one of us is a tragedian, the other a
comedian, I don't know which is which." Indeed, the sheer
perfection of Charlie's rendering of this dance is in danger
of lending sympathy to the character, but the paranoiac
element soon returns when, stamping with rage, Hynkel is
only brought under control when a huge cloak is wrapped
round him. At one moment he pins medals on the great
belly of the drooling Herring, at the next moment, when
things go wrong, he tears them off, snaps the minister's
braces and slaps his face. When Schultz is arrested as a
traitor and Hynkel fails to get from the Jews the money he
needs to invade Austerlich, the full-scale persecution begins.
The little barber finds himself involved in a resistance
movement led by Schultz, who has escaped. Both are in the

end arrested and put in a concentration camp, while Hannah, by now the barber's girl-friend, escapes to Austerlich.

Benzino Napoloni, rival to Hynkel as a fellow dictator, appears to be in opposition to Hynkel's secret plans to take over Austerlich. It is decided to invite him to Tomania and impress him with the nation's strength. Jack Oakie's hammed-up Napoloni is exactly the right foil to Charlie's agile, neurotic Hynkel, and the scene of the meeting of the dictators at the railway station, with all the trouble harassed officials have laying the unrolled carpet at the right coach door to line up with the shunting train, is sheer burlesque, as is the exchange of salutes. Attempts to make the bulging Napoloni feel small entirely fail, and the comedy is developed along more traditional lines in the pantomime which takes place at a military display, at a ball, and during a buffet.

Hynkel goes duck-shooting near the Austerlich border in order to blind the world to his invasion plans, but he finds himself arrested in mistake for the barber, who has escaped with Schultz from the nearby concentration camp. The barber, hiding in the same area, suddenly finds himself taken for the dictator. At first he is terrified by his sudden elevation; troops and tanks sprout from everywhere, and Hannah, now living on a farm, is knocked unconscious. The climax comes when Garbitsch introduces to the microphones the man he assumes to be Hynkel so that he may address the conquered peoples of Austerlich. This, the Jewish barber now realizes, is his greatest opportunity to do service to humanity. At the end of the speech, he addresses himself directly to Hannah, who is seen listening and weeping from happiness as she realizes that it is her lover, not Hynkel, who is speaking in words that reveal his humanity and longing for peace.

This concluding speech was much criticized at the time,

not for its sentiments but because Charlie seemed to step out of character and make his own, personal humanitarian appeal to the world — "We want to live by each other's happiness — not by each other's misery. . . . The way of life can be free and beautiful, but we have lost the way. Greed has poisoned men's souls. . . . More than cleverness, we need kindness and gentleness. . . . soldiers! Don't give yourselves to these brutes — who despise you — enslave you. . . . Let us fight for a new world — a decent world which will give men a chance to work — that will give youth a future and old age a security. . . . Let us fight for a world of reason — a world of science — where progress will lead to the happiness of us all. Soldiers, in the name of democracy, let us unite." He reproduces the speech in full in his autobiography.

The speech is undoubtedly naïve, and Charlie's emotional sincerity spills over. The soldiers he was addressing — those of Nazi Germany and Fascist Italy — were the very ones who would never be allowed to see his film. Charlie explained his outburst in an interview. "I had to do it. They had their laughs. . . . Now I wanted them to listen. . . . I did this picture for the Jews of the world. . . . I'm no Communist . . . just a human being who wants to see this country a real democracy." But the six-minute speech seemed out of context — it did not really suit the little barber, it was too large and universalized, and as a personal appeal from Charlie himself it was largely addressed to audiences who were either already resisting the dictators, or were soon to do so. However, America was not to enter the war until some fourteen months after the initial release of *The Great Dictator* in October 1940, and the film undoubtedly helped to consolidate American opinion against the dictators.

When Charlie showed the film to Harry Hopkins, President Roosevelt's chief adviser, Hopkins said, "It's a great picture, a very worth-while thing to do." When, a little later, he was presented to Roosevelt himself, the President was somewhat less warm, and said, "Your picture is giving us a lot of trouble in the Argentine." Very foolishly, Charlie accepted an invitation to recite the speech over the air from the hall of the Daughters of the American Revolution in Washington. When he felt elements in the audience to be hostile to him, he became suddenly very nervous and dry-mouthed, and he had to call for water in the middle of the recital. This created a lengthy break in the transmission and ruined such effect as the performance might have had. Fortunately, the film itself proved the most successful with the public of any he had made.

The Great Dictator, therefore, initiated the group of films in which Charlie was openly to express his personal feelings on social and, in the broadest sense, political matters. It was not, as we have seen, to help him with that section of the public which was critical of him on political or moral grounds. The difficult years were now to come, and Charlie, in his fifties, began to feel the strain of living in a community which showed increasing signs of active dislike. He kept more and more to himself.

Paulette Goddard had finally left his home in December 1940, while Charlie was in New York. She could take no more, especially after being hard-driven at the studio during the shooting of *The Great Dictator,* where time after time she had had to receive grueling direction in front of the rest of the cast and technicians. She had been constantly driven to tears. She had undoubtedly done her best, and she had been exceptionally good to Charlie's two boys, Charles and Sydney, when they were visiting their father's home. According to Charles, no one regretted her departure more than they did. Paulette remained an established star, and she obtained her divorce quietly in Mexico in 1942.

So in 1941 Charlie again resumed the life of a bachelor. He had also lost one of his closest friends, Douglas Fairbanks, Sr., who had died in 1939. Charlie became increasingly dependent on the presence of the two boys, who were in their middle teens. He was not to release his next film, *Monsieur Verdoux,* until 1947, a gap of seven years. The decade of the 1940s was to be the most severely troubled of his adult life. His problems arose first out of continual allegations concerning his income tax, arising not from evasion on his part but through the excessive claims made by the Tax Department. He had also to cope with growing political troubles, which he exacerbated as the result of his own impulsive and often ill-judged behavior. And thirdly, he had to endure the worst experience of his life in his relations with a girl — Joan Barry's paternity suit against him, which occupied him recurrently from 1943 to 1947.

Politically, the muddy waters of right-wing hysteria continued to be stirred through his ceaseless debate over *The Great Dictator,* and especially over the final speech. Organized Nazi influence in prewar America was at its height, and Charlie continued to be attacked in the right-wing press. With America's precipitate entry into the war following Pearl Harbor in December 1941, the political orientation became even more complicated. America suddenly found herself the ally of Communist Russia, at that time strenuously opposing the onrush of Hitler's armies to the very gates of Moscow and Leningrad, and deep into the Ukraine. The great cry of those not wholly concerned with right-wing isolationism was for a second front to be launched in Europe to break the concentrated Nazi pressure on the Russian armies. Without thinking of possible consequences, Charlie impulsively accepted an invitation given over the telephone by the head of the American Committee for Russian War Relief in San Francisco, urging him to take the place on the platform at a great second-front rally of Joseph E. Davies, the American ambassador to Moscow, who was indisposed. Charlie had accepted in the heat of the moment, but also because he was indignant at the way many

Americans were naïvely hoping that the Germans and Russians would simply wipe each other out and leave the world safe for right-wing democracy. Charlie's audience was ten thousand, and according to his son, he was so nervous he vomited backstage and mislaid what notes he had made to help him through the speech. Consequently, he spoke emotionally for forty minutes, improvising his speech, which he opened with the challenging word "Comrades!" exciting as a result more laughter than applause. Then, after explaining that he meant this on the purely human level ("I am not a Communist, I am a human being"), he worked himself up to an impassioned plea for a second front: "Stalin wants it, Roosevelt has called for it — so let's all call for it — let's open a second front now!" There was wildly enthusiastic applause, and Charlie ended by appealing to everyone present to send a telegram to the President demanding that a second front be opened immediately.

This was in early summer 1942. On July 22 he spoke by telephone for fourteen minutes to a mass meeting of 60,000 trade unionists in Madison Square Garden, New York, again calling emotionally for a second front in an address which opened with the words, "On the battlefield of Russia democracy will live or die." The full text of the address appears in the autobiography. Its style, spoken in urgent, short sentences, is very similar to the speech at the end of *The Great Dictator*. In October 1942 he made a third similar appeal in Carnegie Hall along with Orson Welles and others, followed by another appeal for the Committee for Russian War Relief in the Hotel Pennsylvania. By now he was being warned by friends in Hollywood not to go on with these overemotional speeches, when others were being far more careful what they said. According to his son Charles, he also spoke in New York under the auspices of the Artists Front to Win the War, an organization with a Leftist reputation, and once again he was so nervous that he was sick in the bathroom of his suite in the Waldorf Towers, pacing about in his room while rehearsing the speech. Charles was with him at the time, and comments that hostility to Charlie was building up on the grounds that he gave too little credit to the British for what they were doing in North Africa and in the bombing of Germany, and that he had no right, as a British citizen, to offer advice to Americans as to what they should do. A head of criticism was in fact building up to burst upon him later, and Charlie claims that his social life in the New York area had already become much more restricted as the socialites who used to court him began to avoid his company.

What did burst upon him during the war years was the paternity suit launched by the actress Joan Barry, who had come to him for a test in June 1941 and had eventually been put under contract to the studio at, Charlie says, two hundred and fifty dollars a week. He sent her to the acting school run by Max Reinhardt, the eminent stage director now living in exile in Hollywood. Charlie also coached her himself; apparently she could be momentarily brilliant, but she lacked both self-discipline and concentration as an actress. At this stage, Charlie was considering scripting a new subject, *Shadow and Substance,* based on a play about an Irish girl not unlike a modern Joan of Arc, and he felt that Joan Barry had the talent to play this part. He had bought the screen rights for twenty-five thousand dollars and started work on the script.

Charlie admits that Joan Barry, "a big handsome woman of twenty-two," had attracted him, and that he saw a good deal of her. At the same time, he admits he was uneasy about the strangely persistent way in which she sought his company, turning up unannounced at all hours of the day and night, and then disappearing altogether. She would arrive very drunk, and when he eventually gave orders she should not be admitted, she began to break the windows.

She failed to attend the acting school, and then suddenly decided she did not want to be an actress. She asked for her fare back to New York and five thousand dollars in consideration of canceling her contract. Charlie agreed, thinking he was well rid of her.

But he was not rid of her. When he went to New York to make his second-front speech in Carnegie Hall, she pestered him again to see her, threatening otherwise to commit suicide. She was destitute, she said, and he gave her a further three hundred dollars. When he returned to Beverly Hills, so did she, paying her fare with the money he had given her, and, when he refused to see her, she started once again smashing windows, breaking into the house, demanding money and threatening his life.

All this occurred around Christmas 1942; the boys were home for the holidays, and Charles witnessed his father's consternation. He kept a pistol in his bedroom, and he prowled the house at night looking for intruders. He was afraid that, in her unbalanced state, she would shoot herself in the house in order to implicate him in her death or wounding. Charlie had to send the boys to stay with friends so they would not witness the girl's dangerous hysteria. He put the matter in the hands of the police, but the press was by now alive to the story. Charlie told the police he would pay the girl's fare back to New York in order to prevent her being jailed on a vagrancy charge. According to his son, Charlie was deeply affected by Joan Barry's mental condition, and sincerely wanted to do what he could for her. "She's in love with me, and I'm not in love with her," was what he told his sons by way of simple explanation.

But in May 1943 she returned again, broke into the house, was charged with vagrancy and sentenced to thirty days' detention, most of which she spent under medical care. She claimed she was three months' pregnant, though without mentioning initially who the father was. According to

Charlie, she had been advised to get herself arrested by an unscrupulous press columnist with a nose for a story.

Meanwhile, however, another, and most important interest had entered Charlie's life. This was Oona O'Neill, the seventeen-year-old daughter of the playwright, who was exactly to the month the age of his son Charles. According to Charles, his father had first met her in November 1942, and the attraction between them was deep and mutual, in spite of the great difference in their ages. At the time of their marriage, on June 16, 1943, Charles was fifty-four and Oona eighteen.

Oona had had some professional experience acting in stock, and Charlie had at first considered her as a replacement for Joan Barry in *Shadow and Substance*. He coached her, as he always did his leading ladies. He speaks of her "luminous beauty," her "sequestered charm," her gentleness, her sense of humor, her tolerance. The boys were equally delighted, having hoped, according to Charles, to date her themselves before they realized the nature of their father's preoccupation with her. According to Charles, she worshipped his father. He describes her as quiet, quick to be amused, with an elfin quality, friendly but shy, and with an intelligence which was half-concealed and a maturity beyond her years. Her mother, with whom she lived along with her stepfather, had separated from Eugene O'Neill when her daughter was only two, and there had been little contact between father and daughter.

The paternity suit filed by Joan Barry against Charlie came at almost the same time as Charlie's secret marriage. According to Charles, his father had categorically refused to settle out of court and so keep the matter, as far as possible, away from the press. He knew he was innocent, and he preferred to fight the matter out in public, though his various acts of charity to the demented girl could be twisted against him by strict application of the Californian law. The ex-

pected press avalanche had burst — vilification of Charlie
for having the mother of *his* child arrested, leaving her
destitute, and so forth. From the beginning of June 1943
Charlie had been living with friends in hiding from the
press; it was to this hiding place that Oona came. Her
mother stood by her decision to marry Charlie, but since
she was now eighteen she no longer required parental con-
sent had her father, Eugene O'Neill, wanted to step in and
prevent the marriage. In effect, they eloped to Santa Barbara
in order to avoid the reporters, arriving at the courthouse at
nine in the morning to obtain the necessary license to marry.
Harry Crocker, now with the Hearst press, made all the
advance arrangements and saw Charlie, nervous and with
his hand shaking, go through the business of signing and
sealing. The license secured, the couple were married by the
Justice of the Peace at Carpinteria, fifteen miles from Santa
Barbara. According to Charlie, there was a wild, Keystone-
like dash by car, when they were chased by the press all the
way to Carpinteria. They finally evaded the press cars in the
back streets of Santa Barbara, where their honeymoon was
to be spent.

When she heard about Charlie's marriage, Joan Barry
went into hysteria, and the press was unanimous in con-
demnation of Charlie. The rest of the summer was spent
preparing the defense against the paternity suit, which was
a civil case. Attempts were made by the lawyers to induce
Joan Barry to agree to a blood test after the child was born;
she agreed to drop the paternity suit if the test were negative, but she wanted $25,000 to agree to the test. However,
this could only happen after the birth of the child, who
proved to be a daughter, born on October 3, 1943. Meanwhile, pending the paternity suit, Charlie had to pay heavily
($10,000 in the first year) for the maintenance of the child,
as if it were his own.

Charlie had been warned that certain influential politicians were out to "get him," and indeed the federal government initiated a grand jury investigation into Charlie's case under the Mann Act, which prohibited the transportation of women from one state to another for immoral purposes. Charlie was eventually indicted on four counts and so threatened, if found guilty, with a sentence of up to twenty years' imprisonment. Even when the blood test was finally taken, and Charlie was proven not to have been the father of Joan Barry's child, the federal case against him still had to proceed.

The charges were ludicrous; that, because he had paid Joan Barry's fare to and from New York, he was guilty of white slavery under the Mann Act, and that he had sought to deprive her of her civil rights by procuring her deportation from California. After the preliminary hearing, the photographers burst in when Charlie was being fingerprinted, which was strictly against regulations. Yet no effort was made to prevent it. From January to April 1944, when Charlie was finally acquitted on all counts, the press had a gala feast at his expense.

The trial itself started in March and lasted ten days. Joan Barry took the stand and gave her own lurid account of her intimacy with Charlie. Charlie, taking the oath, denied her descriptions, but admitted there had been a romance in the early days of their relationship. The evidence produced by many witnesses revealed the unbalanced state of Joan Barry's mind and the troubled conditions of her life. The jury after prolonged deliberation (held up, apparently, by a single hostile woman) pronounced Charlie not guilty. Even then, he was not left entirely free. Another lawyer, hostile to Charlie, had the paternity case reopened in 1946. By this time, the guardianship of Joan Barry's child had been transferred to the court. The jury disagreed, and yet another trial had to be held, after which, in spite of the negative blood test, Charlie was ordered to support the child, paying seventy-five and later one hundred dollars a week. Miss Barry was later to get married, a marriage which was unfortunately to collapse.

The subject of *Monsieur Verdoux* was originally suggested to Charlie by Orson Welles. Welles had made the proposition that Charlie might care to play the notorious French murderer, Landru, in a wholly serious film he intended to make. On reflection, Charlie decided he wanted to develop a comedy around this character, and bought out the idea from Welles for the sum of five thousand dollars and a screen credit, "Idea suggested by Orson Welles."

Charlie was to ponder the script for this controversial film for some two years, eventually putting it into production only in June 1946. He made it unusually fast; it was only twelve weeks in production. This shows up technically in the film, though Totheroh had the help of two other directors of photography. Nevertheless, the costs were relatively high, around two million dollars, a great deal of personal money to risk on a subject of this kind, in which Charlie transformed himself into a precise, dapper, and highly professional murderer for money, whose attitude to the way of life he had chosen reflects the cynicism of the capitalist world, as he sees it. There is no trace of psychological morbidity in the treatment of the character; the irony lies entirely in the broader social theme Charlie is developing — that if, as Clausewitz once put it, diplomacy leads to war, the cutthroat competition of the business world leads logically to murder. Verdoux is simply a businessman whose formal profession is marriage to and murder of elderly widows or spinsters in order to inherit their money; in return he flatters them and makes them happy for a brief while before he kills them. Charlie plays Verdoux on the contrasting note of ironic ruthlessness and emotional sensitivity — the poet-villain. But Verdoux is far too complex a character to engage the sympathies of the mass audience, which is what the evolution of the tramp character from his beginning to *Modern Times* had invariably done, and which the little barber had managed to sustain in *The Great Dictator*. The appeal of *Monsieur Verdoux* (for those to whom it does appeal) lies in the challenge Verdoux's philosophy poses to the intelligence, and not in its emotional qualities. It is Charlie's closest approach to uncompromising satire.

The film was finally released in April 1947, but only after considerable trouble with the American film industry censorship, the Breen Office of the Motion Picture Association, which, on seeing the script, was inclined initially to ban it. In his autobiography, Charlie quotes from the letters he received from the Breen Office and the passages that offended them in the script of the film. The letters from the Breen Office raised objection in passing to the recurrent indictment of the "System" in the film, as if this had some sinister political significance, but concentrated on the nature of the views expressed by Verdoux to explain his attitude to his crimes as the primary ground for the unacceptable nature of the film. They then added, somewhat gratuitously, that there was a "distasteful flavor of illicit sex" about the film to which they must also raise objection. Charlie records his discussion with Breen himself, and his resistance to the modifications Breen wanted introduced to lines or inferences which nowadays would pass utterly unnoticed. But this was 1947, the year in which the Committee on Un-American Activities was to make its first, devastating appearance in Hollywood. However, the Breen Office finally passed the picture.

Mary Pickford accompanied Oona and Charlie to the first night in New York. The press was politely hostile during interviews, and many were antagonistic in their reviews — though not such notables as Lewis Jacobs or James Agee.

The audience included people who had come to hiss, and others who had come to applaud and laugh, as Charlie puts it, more as a challenge than as a genuine response to the film's satiric humor. It was an uneasy experience for Charlie, and he left his seat during the projection, wandering about to various parts of the house to test audience reaction.

The public response to *Monsieur Verdoux* was less than for any Chaplin film so far. It was barred in some cities and in many theaters, and received in the United States less than one-sixth the distribution of his previous, popular films. It was better received in Europe, but not by the mass audience. It had to be faced that, brilliant as the film often was, it was wholly alien to the public's conception of Charlie. The atmosphere was more like that in a play by Bernard Shaw, or even a fable by Swift or Voltaire, and the style of the dialogue, as can be seen from the extracts published in the autobiography, is somewhat mannered. But, as in virtually all Charlie's feature films, the element of fable supervenes over the element of realism. Fable permits the underlining of themes at the expense of wholly naturalistic action and situation. The demand for sheer naturalism is as misplaced in relation to a film like *Monsieur Verdoux* as it would be to, say, *Major Barbara* or *The Apple Cart*. But the dialogue is scarcely always "at ease" within its own conceptual level of writing, while the acting, deployment and movement of the characters is sometimes awkward. This is immediately noticeable in the grouping of the opening sequence, which is like that of an inferior stock company, giving the film an awkward and off-putting start. The technique throughout is very simple, avoiding all the fashionable contemporary Hollywood technique Charlie so much despised. He disliked close-ups, except for very specific moments; as a pantomimist, he wanted his hands, his body, his feet to be visible. His French assistant for the film, Robert Florey, in his book *Hollywood d'hier et d'aujourd'hui,* has described with the critical sympathy of a friend the difficulties to be faced when working with Charlie after years directing more conventional Hollywood productions.

There are many moments of high comedy in *Monsieur Verdoux* — Verdoux showing the wealthy Mme. Grosnay around the house where he had just murdered his latest "wife" and behaving with the aplomb of the perfect salesman who turns into the perfect suitor the moment he learns she is a widow; the burlesque love scenes with the indestructible Martha Raye; the reception where two of the intended victims are unfortunately present at the same social event and have to be outmaneuvered. And there are overtones of pathos within the romantic irony of the scenes between Verdoux and the disillusioned girl (Marilyn Nash) whom he had originally intended to poison. She is saved from destruction at his hands because she represents a kind of balanced optimism. And kindness, even romance, though again treated ironically, lies in the relationship of Verdoux to his crippled wife and child, whom he constantly revisits and treats with the greatest tenderness.

But the film moves inevitably toward a climax in which its purpose becomes more serious, and the dialogue aphoristic with suggestion. The true Verdoux, a simple, humane, sensitive man in accord with the Chaplin tradition, has been soured by society; his secure job gone, he takes to crime, living on the black market of his wits, murdering eccentric old ladies after giving them a few moments of unexpected happiness when they think they have found a new "husband." But he kills with the same ruthless efficiency with which a soldier is trained to kill in battle. He has been dehumanized by the cruelty which he has found active in contemporary competitive society, alike in war as in peace. When he loses through some catastrophe the family he loves, and for whom he labors, the final bitterness enters his soul; he allows himself to be arrested and tried for murder. After the death sentence is passed, he says, "I shall see you all very soon," implying that society in destroying him is in the process of destroying itself. He tells the press, when a reporter seeks an interview with him in his cell, that "crime does not pay in a small way," that robbery and murder are the natural expression of "these criminal times. . . . One murder makes a villain, a million a hero." When the priest comes to escort him to his execution, he says, "I am at peace with God; my conflict is with man." And when the priest prays for mercy on his soul, he adds, "Why not; after all, it belongs to him." In the earlier films, the end was the road to the future; in *Monsieur Verdoux* the end is the way to extermination. Charlie still thinks highly of this film in spite of his early claims for *The Gold Rush*. He says in his autobiography, "I believe *Monsieur Verdoux* is the cleverest and most brilliant film I have yet made."

After making *Monsieur Verdoux*, Charlie again relapsed into comparative inactivity. Domestically he was now far happier than he had ever been; his roster of children by Oona began to mount. His daughter Geraldine was born in 1944; his son Michael John in 1946; his daughters Victoria and Josephine in 1949 and 1951. At the studio, however, things were scarcely the same. Harry Bergman, his longest-lasting associate, died in 1946. His studio manager, Alfred Reeves, with links going back to the Karno days, died in the same year; while Charlie's close friend and neighbor, Dr. Cecil Reynolds, the surgeon, committed suicide.

Charlie had the same right as anyone else to his political views. What caused him so much trouble was his indiscreet, public assertion of this right, though often in the form of admirable loyalties — such as his support, on the basis of friendship, not politics, of such left-wing artists as the composer Hanns Eisler, whose deportation was ordered after he had appeared as an "unfriendly" witness in the Hollywood Un-American Activities inquiry in 1947. Charlie had in November been reported in *Les Lettres Françaises* as having requested Picasso (an avowed Communist, as everyone knew) to form a committee to protest on Eisler's behalf. There were hints dropped during the period of the 1947 investigations that Charlie would himself be subpoenaed as an unfriendly witness, and he has revealed in his autobiography that during the final editing stages of *Monsieur Verdoux* he was indeed informed he would be requested to answer for himself in Washington. He assured them, he says, "I am not a Communist, neither have I ever joined any political party or organization in my life." Although he was never to be summoned, his name was linked by some "friendly" witnesses with the Left. He was accused in certain right-wing journals of being "a card-carrying member of the Communist Party for many years."

Such allegations were sufficient for him to be frozen out of Hollywood society. People did not bother to ascertain the truth; the smear in itself was enough. His deportation was demanded by a speaker in Congress in June 1947, who asked that his "loathsome pictures" be kept from corrupting the eyes of American youth. His long association with radicals was not forgotten. He also gave his public support to Henry Wallace, who had been strongly critical of Truman's anti-Soviet policy and ran as Progressive Party candidate for the presidency in 1947, cooperation with the Soviet Union being part of his platform. Charlie himself records the rough reception given him by the press when he held a conference in New York in connection with the premiere of *Monsieur Verdoux* in April 1947. James Agee had the courage to stand up for Charlie during this conference. In some states the film was picketed by organizations such as the American Legion or the Catholic Legion, and circuit bookings were canceled.

A factor in American public opinion which had told against Charlie was his failure to take out American citizenship. Huff quotes him as making statements such as, "I am not a Jew. I am a citizen of the world"; "I am not a Communist; I am a peace-monger." Charlie had been resident in the United States for some thirty-five years, but he still remained a British citizen.

Living in virtual isolation in Hollywood, Charlie spent his last years in America planning and making *Limelight* (1952). Work on this began late in 1951. In his autobiography, Charlie says the original idea for *Limelight* came when he witnessed the loss of intimate contact with his audience experienced by the comedian Frank Tinney, who had once been a great favorite at the Winter Gardens in New York, but who had entirely lost his touch when Charlie saw him at some later date. This made him wonder what could bring about such a change; he adds that in Calvero's case in *Limelight* it is age combined with too much dignity and introspection.

Limelight was an essay in nostalgia, and a reaffirmation of the values Charlie had learned from his mother and from his personal experience in the English music halls before 1910, in the old world of entertainment, during the late Victorian and Edwardian eras of his youth. To make it he gathered around him as many of his familiars as he could — his half-brother Wheeler Dryden, his son Sydney, and his fellow clowns who knew the period as well as he did, Snub Pollard, Norman Lloyd and, as an inspired choice, Buster Keaton, who had fallen on hard times since his great days in the 1920s. He devised the choreography for the film with the principal dancers who appeared in it, Melissa Hayden and André Eglevsky. With the help of Ray Rasch he composed the three songs he sings in the film: "The Animal Trainer," "The Sardine Song," and "Spring Is Here." Behind the camera were Karl Struss and Rollie Totheroh. But neither

Harry Bergman nor Alfred Reeves was there to see this last production in Hollywood through; Robert Aldrich, however, acted as his assistant director before going on to become a major director in his own right. Outside the studio the world was frozen; no one interested in preserving his name with the authoritarians of Hollywood cared to be seen in Charlie's company.

For his new leading lady Charlie chose Claire Bloom, the most sensitive actress ever to play opposite him, with her calm and immaculate beauty and her dancer's elegance of movement. She is Terry, the dancer with the hysterical obsession that she has lost the use of her legs, which is surely Charlie's evocation of his mother, whose voice had failed her before she finally lost her reason. Charlie plays Calvero, the once-famous comedian who seeks solace in alcohol, as Charlie's father had done. Charlie's son Sydney appears as Neville, the young composer, while another of his sons, Charles Junior, plays a clown in the ballet, and three of his and Oona's small children also appear momentarily. For setting, Charlie recreates in the simplest possible form the streets of London as he had known them — the back projections are only too obvious, but somehow do not matter, for the film stands like a kind of loving anachronism among the productions of 1951. It is not so much a fable as an elegiac poem to the faded glories of music hall in contrast to the strident spectacles of the contemporary stage musical.

The film opens with a 1920s caption: "The glamor of Limelight, from which age must fade as youth enters." Of the streets Charlie comments, "All the world's a stage, and this one is the most legitimate." Even the stage manager, Mr. Postant, is named after William Postance, who managed the Duke of York's Theatre where Charlie had played in *Sherlock Holmes*. The whole conduct of the action, its precise, explicit, almost Dickensian narration, spoken by Charlie himself, its sentimental melodrama of the old clown dying as the youthful dancer achieves her stardom, belong to the age of the moral tale rather than the harsher realities of the midtwentieth-century film of action.

In his lodgings in one of the shabby-genteel areas of London, an imaginary Kennington, Calvero adopts the young girl Terry, a dancer who has tried to take her life before she has ever learned how to win a public for her art. She lies paralyzed until Calvero is able to revive her desire for life and art. But Calvero's own failure is brought home to him by a single engagement he manages to obtain, and the roles are reversed. It is Terry's affection which keeps the old man in heart. She becomes a star; but in spite of the affection they feel for each other, Calvero instinctively realizes she should marry the young composer Neville, who is in love with her. So he quietly withdraws from her life, and becomes a street musician. She rediscovers him, and organizes a benefit show for him. Working with a fellow clown as partner (Keaton), Calvero provides the climax of the show, and they are a sensational success. But it is too late; Calvero is old and frail, and the excitement proves too great. He dies in the wings as Terry goes on to dance.

Perhaps *Limelight* should have been Charlie's last film. It is a near-perfect work of art in the tradition of the swan song, made as Charlie puts it himself, in "the elegant melancholy of twilight." Charlie was able to speak in his own right, to enact a role created to express his positive philosophy, just as *Monsieur Verdoux* expressed his bitterness. As for his talent, this is represented by the crowning appearance at the end of the film of the two master comedians of the 1920s — Charlie and Buster Keaton. Together for three minutes they recreate the whole art of the comic sketch as it was at the turn of the century.

After *Limelight* was completed in 1952, Charlie and Oona decided to go abroad on a six-month vacation. It was not their intention at this stage to leave the United States forever; they had recently renovated and extended their home. Charlie's request as a British national for a reentry permit to the United States led to prolonged stalling by the U.S. authorities. He was interrogated by a team from the Immigration Office, and in the end granted a reentry permit. After launching *Limelight* in New York, Charlie and Oona left for Europe with their family on the liner *Queen Elizabeth* on September 17, 1952. Only when they were on board ship did a cable arrive stating the Attorney General had rescinded the reentry permit, and that Charlie could not return to the United States without facing an Immigration Board of Inquiry, "to answer charges of a political nature and of moral turpitude." Charlie was officially declared by the Attorney General himself to be a person of "unsavory character" against whom the Department hinted darkly they had new evidence. Meanwhile, the FBI was ordered to give the Chaplin case a further investigation. However, no public hearing was ever held.

The withdrawal of his permit to reenter the United States after he had left American shores was a bitter blow to Charlie. He made no attempt to defend his position, and he was not to return to the country which meant so much to him until 1972, twenty years later.

SEVEN

Manoir de Ban
The Halcyon Years

EUROPE DID ITS BEST to salve the psychological wounds with which Charlie and Oona had left the United States. London received him with its usual popular acclaim; naturally he took Oona on the obligatory visit to Kennington.

The worry in the forefront of Charlie's mind was his fortune, which remained deposited in the United States. Soon after reaching London, Oona, who retained her American citizenship and her passport, was forced to return to California to negotiate the transference of Charlie's deposits from the United States to Europe. She found that the FBI had already interrogated their domestic staff. But the removal of Charlie's capital from the United States was not blocked.

The family finally settled in Switzerland; Charlie bought the thirty-seven-acre estate of Manoir de Ban in the village of Corsair near Vevey on Lake Geneva. Five acres of this estate is a lawn shaded by fine trees through which the mountain scenery and the lake below can be seen. They have lived there permanently since 1954. Oona, who was eventually to give up her American citizenship, was to have

four more children, making her family eight in all. Charlie
was in his early seventies when his last child was born.

Charlie, aged sixty-five in 1954, brooded on his misadventures. They rankled bitterly, and finally precipitated themselves in the film he made at Shepperton Studios in England
during 1956, *A King in New York.* It is interesting for
the nature of its comment on the United States, then at
the climax of its problems with Senator McCarthy and the
prolonged phases in the successive investigations by the
Un-American Activities Committees of the House of Representatives, which filled the press at home and abroad.
Investigations in Hollywood had begun as early as 1947;
though McCarthy himself was never to interrogate the
motion picture industry, successive committees during the
1950s issued subpoenas to "unfriendly" witnesses in every
branch of entertainment.

If Charlie had conceived *A King in New York* in terms
similar to those of *Monsieur Verdoux,* he might have
achieved a second satire on the theme of modern in-
tolerance, and a film of at least comparable stature. But he
let a measure of personal rancor intrude into the film, and
turned this likely theme into the most didactic and least
inspired of his major films. *A King in New York* tells the
story of a certain King Shahdov of Estrovia who is displaced
following a revolution. He arrives penniless as a refugee in
New York, estranged from his wife (who seeks asylum in
Europe) and supported only by his country's ambassador to
the United States. He has come to America because he
believes it to be a land inspired by ideals of freedom and
youthful vitality, but he is rapidly disillusioned. Spurred on
by mounting debts, he allows himself to be exploited on
television by appearing in lucrative commercials. In this he
is helped by a beautiful girl acting for an advertising
agency, who sees in his royal highness an alluring oppor-

tunity to combine business with seduction. He does not
prove an ideal advertiser, since he develops aversions to
some of the products, and ends by attacking the glamorizing
process of plastic surgery, the principles of big business, and
even rock and roll.

He befriends a ten-year-old boy, Rupert, a child prodigy,
whose parents are caught up in one of the Un-American
Activities Committee investigations. The boy's reaction has
been to run away from school, and the Committee decides
to probe into Shahdov's political associations. He is ordered
to appear before the Committee, and is finally cleared —
but not before he has slipped into slapstick and accidentally
doused the investigators with a fire hose in which his finger
gets stuck on his way to the committee room. In the circumstances, he decides the only thing he can do is leave for
Europe, and seek some kind of reconciliation with his
Queen. Before he goes, he visits Rupert, who has returned
again to school, and discovers the child has been broken by
the investigators and forced to inform on his parents' political associates. The boy is in a desperate state; his natural
independence of character appears to have been destroyed.
Shahdov, deeply affected, tries to explain that the true spirit
of America will one day shine through and dissolve the
clouds which presently obscure it.

It is easy to trace the revival of old themes in this film —
the echoes of *The Kid,* the susceptibility of an older man to
the charms of a young woman; or memories of *The Immigrant,* when Shahdov, excited by his arrival in America,
makes an emotional speech about his feelings at the very
moment his fingerprints are being taken. But the film basically fails to fire because it has been conceived in the spirit
of didacticism rather than ironic or satiric comedy. Certainly, there are episodes that are funny — for example, the
sequence of Shahdov trying to dodge the writ server, an
experience Charlie had once undergone in real life. Whereas

there is a certain elemental splendor to the "homespun" philosophy of the final speech in *The Great Dictator,* and subtlety in the irony which gives *Monsieur Verdoux* a "universal" quality in its idealistic comment on contemporary society, *A King in New York* fails to ignite a similar flame. Shahdov, in fact, is a character of insufficient stature or universal appeal to sustain the level of humanitarian significance that Charlie is trying to impose on him. He merely preaches the message he should embody.

However, Charlie had attempted to create yet another fable for our times conceived in terms of an old-fashioned, oversentimental idealism. In Dawn Addams he found a lively and attractive leading lady, and in his son Michael a more than eager and adequate child actor as the boy Rupert. He worked on the film for weeks on end, perfecting the acting performances and, at times, driving his artists and collaborators to despair that they could ever achieve what he was demanding of them. Once again, he composed his own music, often skillfully integrated with the action, and once again the sets look barely adequate.

During the years preceding its publication in 1964, Charlie set himself the difficult task of compiling his life story in the book he entitled *My Autobiography.* This was difficult for many reasons, which this remarkable book readily reveals. Charlie is at once a very secret and a very public man; his enjoyment in performance and his delight and even wonder at his phenomenal success and public acclaim demand that he write about himself and present a public image commensurate with his unique degree of fame. He needs constant recognition and acclaim to remind him that the whole thing is not a dream, like the dreams he has introduced into so many of his films. All this demands expression, even assertion and reassertion.

But at the same time, Charlie has been forced to live the

more painful episodes of his private life in a blaze of often prurient publicity which tormented him and increased his deep and natural desire to withdraw forever from the public eye. But even in this tortured area in his experience, there are the occasional marks of the showman who is not averse to letting the world know he is a Lothario, a Don Juan, but one who has been nevertheless an easy prey for women given to duplicity. His romantic, at times Dickensian conception of women only too readily slips from the sphere of delusory admiration into suspicion and reaction. His accounts of his various relationships with women are fairly well rationalized from the male point of view.

The outstanding section of the autobiography is the first part which deals with his early life in London — his childhood in Kennington, his youth in the theater, his work for Karno in England and the United States. His account of London at the turn of the century almost rivals that of Dickens's London of half a century and more earlier. A whole society, now long past, is pictured through the eyes of an isolated child. But as he becomes more successful the book begins to fail as a continuous story, saying less and less about his films — with the notable exception of *Monsieur Verdoux* — and more about his social life insofar as this reflects his phenomenal success. The story becomes more sketchy, more anecdotal, more superficial even, as if increasingly Charlie has no real experience to relate once his steps towards a firm and established success have been evaluated. The few pages devoted to the years of persecution read as if he had to court disaster to prove to himself the utter impregnability of his success — a dangerous, even masochistic experiment in living, which extends as well to his relations with women. Gradually his male uncertainty about them is revealed, is in effect rationalized. About his marriage to Lita Grey, the mother of two of his sons Charlie, Jr., and Sydney, he chooses to say nothing at all.

In his account of his political problems he is revealing only to the point of showing his naïveté. He lays himself open to the troubles which descended on him with increasing venom at a period when the United States was peculiarly sensitive and bigoted in its refusal to see the elemental humanity and goodwill which prompted his public statements and political stance. He had the right to select his friends where he would, and many of them were undoubtedly Leftists. This became a stick with which to beat the man who had done so much to foster humanity in his films.

Charlie's autobiography reveals his basic, Anglo-American snobbishness about meeting the titled and socially famous, as well as the heads of states who welcome him to their countries and decorate him with their honors. The contacts are often of the slightest, and amount to little more than name-dropping. Of greater value are his accounts of more established friendships with people of outstanding character, such as H. G. Wells or Max Eastman, or his closest friend of all among the famous, Douglas Fairbanks, Sr.

So the autobiography falls far short of "telling all." It begins like a masterpiece, and declines into a miscellany of anecdote from which it is possible to glean something of value from time to time toward understanding Charlie's philosophy of life, a self-evolved philosophy which he has tested in the hardest of all ways — against the prevailing tastes of audiences, who have responded to it for decades with warmth and affection, but also against hardheaded authority which, in times of stress, has viewed him increasingly as a self-indulgent, undesirable, sex-obsessed, left-wing alien. Charlie, expatriate from a Britain which had little to offer him, was forced to become an exile from the United States which had given him so much until they finally denied him the basic human rights without which he could not function either as a man or as an artist.

Charlie's last film was to be an old-fashioned comedy of modest pretensions and entertainment value. This was *A Countess from Hong Kong* (1966), made in Britain. Charlie was now seventy-seven, and he makes only a single, momentary, Hitchcock-like appearance. This is as a ship's steward. Otherwise, the film is remarkable only for the celebrity of its cast, bringing together Marlon Brando and Sophia Loren as the principals, and adding Margaret Rutherford in a beautiful, vignette performance and Patrick Cargill, who acts everyone else off the screen as the comically devoted British manservant who never fails to carry out his master's absurdest demands.

But this striking combination of the screen's most talked-of actor and arguably the screen's most beautiful actress leads to little but a charade in the tired tradition of the oldest-fashioned bedroom farce. It is the story of an American millionaire, Ogden, who unwillingly acquires the companionship of a certain Natascha, a beautiful but penniless Russian emigré countess whom he meets casually in Hong Kong and who decides to stowaway in his stateroom when his ship sails. Although he wishes to be rid of her so that he can take up an offer of an ambassadorship without embarrassment, he gradually comes to care for her, and makes his manservant marry her in order that she may enter the United States, since she has no passport or documents of identity. The film consists largely of frenetic concealments as stewards and other intruders enter Ogden's suite. The film ends romantically with Ogden preferring a life with Natascha to reconciliation with his estranged wife and career as ambassador. Had not Charlie directed the film, and Marlon Brando and Sophia Loren appeared in it, *A Countess from Hong Kong* would scarcely have been noticed among the films of its year. Its entertainment value lies entirely in the past. Although Sophia Loren works hard, Brando appears only ill-at-ease and disgruntled; the dialogue is mannered and self-conscious, and the whole film seems labored in conception, enlivened only by the resilient performance by Patrick Cargill. Charlie's true swan song remains *Limelight;* the critical and public reception alike for *A Countess from Hong Kong* was unfavorable.

Nevertheless, Charlie's mood in old age appears to be a happy one, living in great domestic comfort with his much-beloved family on his beautiful estate in Switzerland. He has occupied himself composing music for his old silent films, such as *The Kid* and *The Idle Class* (of which he supervised the recordings in London), and *The Circus,* for which he also composed a special theme song.* And he has worked on scripts for films to be made, if his wishes are carried out, after his death.

Two major events have gladdened his old age. First was a grand-scale retrospective presentation of his films and a great celebration staged in his honor during the Venice Film Festival in 1972, and second, his tour of reconciliation in the United States the previous spring, during which all former differences appear to have been forgiven, perhaps because a new generation, more enlightened, or "permissive," had taken over from the generation which had banished him. His brief return to America was on the eve of his eighty-third birthday.

The United States was to make its peace with Charlie on

---

* In 1971, Charlie agreed to the rerelease of nine of his feature films, leasing them for a period of fifteen years for a reputed six million dollars, plus a percentage. In the same year Black Ink Films acquired the world television rights to Charlie's films for a sum said to run into many million dollars. In 1972, the British Broadcasting Corporation paid Black Ink £250,000 for the British rights to televise Charlie's films, including carefully restored versions of the early shorts, screened, naturally, at their correct speed, and set to music. American television paid five million dollars for nine of his major films, plus half the profits. The year 1972 also saw the rerelease of *Modern Times* in Europe, followed by *Limelight.* The original negatives of Charlie's films are being stored in a wine cellar at his house; the cellar has been specially adapted for film preservation with temperature and humidity control. Charlie's personal fortune in 1972 was estimated at $15 million.

April 5, 1972. There, at the Lincoln Center in New York, he received a three-minute standing ovation from an audience of twenty-eight hundred who had come to see him and his films, *The Idle Class* and *The Kid*. A champagne buffet at one hundred dollars a head followed the screening. Charlie blew kisses to his emotionally demonstrative audience. He had come back to the United States for the first time since 1952, to receive, on April 10, a special Oscar award from the Motion Picture Academy in Los Angeles.

The following September he appeared in Venice at a mass open-air screening of *City Lights* in the Piazza San Marco, and was received with cheers by thousands of people when he stood at a window overlooking the piazza. Later that evening the Italian President presented him with a commemorative statuette of the Golden Lion of St. Mark at a ceremony held in the magnificently decorated late eighteenth-century La Fenice theater. He looked well, but very frail, scarcely able to stand following a bad fall in his house. He said nothing, but smiled and gestured kisses to the audience of film notables who had come to the festival from every part of the world, and who gave him a standing ovation lasting minutes. We knew, as we looked at him standing on the forefront of the stage waving and blowing kisses, that this was most probably his final public appearance. It was fitting that those who stood to pay him honor were his successors as filmmakers, directors, stars and creative workers in the film industry he had done so much to establish as the great new art of the twentieth century through his unsparing and devoted work over a period which had exceeded fifty years.

It is not easy to decide the relative position Charlie's films occupy today in the ever-changing perspective of taste in contemporary world entertainment. In a sense, his reputa-

tion has suffered from its very greatness, much as the reputations of Bernard Shaw and H. G. Wells still suffer. Their
immense achievements are part of the warp and woof of the
earlier decades of the twentieth century; to a considerable
degree, they created as well as reflected and interpreted a
period with which the younger generations today feel little
contact. However, in Charlie's case there is no doubt that his
earliest and least demanding films, with their mixture of
balletic slapstick, set sequences of brilliant comic pantomime, and human touches of pathos have an immediate
and timeless appeal for all age groups, even though their
backgrounds — urban slums and other environments — their
costumes, makeup, and supporting characterizations, are
now completely "dated." But they are films that require the
immediate, infectious laughter of a live audience, the
laughter they were intended to inspire. They are far less
successful on television, viewed "cold" in the living room
on a small screen with comic, or pseudocomic musical ac-
companiment. The action, often spread over twenty minutes
or more, can seem in these circumstances slow and the gags
repetitive. On the other hand, sympathetically introduced
and presented with the simplest of piano accompaniments
and the laughter of a "participating" audience, selected
highlights from Charlie's earlier films can be successful even
on television. But it would seem that their future lies almost
entirely in the field of nontheatrical distribution to film
societies and the like rather than in the theaters or on
television.

Fine as the best of these earlier films are, they were completely overtaken by Charlie's work from the period of *The
Kid* to *Limelight*. He has, as we have seen, added a sound
track to the key silent films carrying music and in some instances a narration spoken by himself. But even with these
additions, the silent masterpieces are likely to draw audi-

ences to the art houses and specialized cinemas rather than to the more highly competitive theaters showing the latest features.

Indeed, Charlie's finest work, like that of most men of genius in part overtaken by time, becomes increasingly appreciated by the buffs, the enthusiasts, the connoisseurs and the students of cinema. Fortunately, these are felt to exist in substantial numbers, as evidenced by the high prices paid for the long-term distribution rights to Charlie's principal works. Indeed, Charlie may well gain rather than lose by the passage of time, becoming more and more a period genius, like Dickens, rather than a great artist identified with a span in the century held to be merely "out-of-date." The people prepared to view Charlie's films in the context of the times in which they were created — whether or not they were themselves alive in these times with direct experience to draw upon — are the people who stand to gain most from seeing and reseeing the greater films. Just as Buster Keaton, Charlie's closest rival now as a perfectionist creative artist in the film comedy of the 1920s, has excited a great revival of interest among the connoisseurs, so Charlie, an artist who in the end stands for a much wider range of achievement than Keaton, should never lose his appeal, and indeed should from now on increase it. It was Buster Keaton's utter lack of sentimentality as well as his marvelous comic inventiveness and technical command which led to his partial eclipse of Charlie among the intellectuals of the cinema during the 1960s.

Charlie Chaplin possessed undoubted genius during the prolonged period of his creativity, stretching from his embryonic work in 1914 at least to the period of *Limelight* in 1952. This already exceeds the span of Dickens's major work from the time of *Pickwick Papers* (1836) to the unfinished novel *Edwin Drood* (1870). While it would be unrealistic to compare the work of these two very different artists of the highest order who worked in very different media, it would not perhaps be unfair to say that Chaplin has occupied much the same place in the hearts of the people of the twentieth century that Dickens occupied in the nineteenth, and that, because he was working in a new and internationalized visual medium, his public during the height of his success has been incomparably larger in numbers. If there is any creative artist with whom Charlie might care to be classed, it is probably Dickens. It seems to me right to do so.

Selected Bibliography
and Suggestions for
Further Reading

Agee, James. *Agee on Film*. New York: McDowell, 1958; London: Peter Owen, 1963.

For perceptive criticism in a series of articles on *Monsieur Verdoux,* and for the article "Comedy's Greatest Era."

Bazin, André. *What Is Cinema?* Vol. II. Berkeley: University of California Press, 1971.

For Bazin's detailed review of *Limelight*.

Brownlow, Kevin. *The Parade's Gone By*. New York: Knopf; London: Secker and Warburg, 1968.

For its detailed, affectionate recreation of the American cinema during the 1920s, and its special references to Chaplin.

Chaplin, Charles. *Charlie Chaplin's Own Story*. Indianapolis: Bobbs-Merrill, 1916.

A collector's item; recollections which are as much invention as fact.

My Wonderful Visit. London: Hurst and Blackett, 1922; published in the United States as *My Trip Abroad,* New York: Harper, 1922.

An ingenuous account of Chaplin's visit to Europe.

My Autobiography. London: The Bodley Head, 1964. New York: Simon and Schuster, 1964. New York: Pocket Books, 1966. London: Penguin Books, 1966.

Chaplin's account of his life as recollected in old age.

Chaplin, Charles, Jr. *My Father.* New York: Random House, 1960.

Recollections by Chaplin's son, particularly relating to the 1930s. Sympathetic and useful for domestic detail.

Cotes, Peter, and Niklaus, Thelma. *The Little Fellow.* London: Paul Elek, 1951; New York: Citadel, 1965.

The latter edition updated. This is a pleasant, informal analysis of Chaplin's career.

Delluc, Louis. *Charlie Chaplin.* Translated by Hamish Miles. London: The Bodley Head, 1922.

Delluc's essay was one of the first sustained analyses of Chaplin's work.

Eastman, Max. *Enjoyment of Laughter.* London: Hamish Hamilton, 1937. *Great Companions.* New York: Farrar, Straus, and Cudahy, 1959.

An impression of Chaplin by one of his closest friends; Chaplin's personal assessment of humor is discussed in the light of Eastman's own philosophy of the comic.

Huff, Theodore. *Charlie Chaplin.* New York: Henry Schuman, 1951; London: Cassell, 1952.

Although limited by its date, this remains the most authoritative account of Chaplin's life and the most thorough analysis of his films.

Jacobs, Lewis. *The Rise of the American Film.* New York: Harcourt, Brace, 1939.

Still very much a standard work on the subject, with Chaplin's work seen in perspective.

Lahue, Kalton C. *Mack Sennett's Keystone.* South Brunswick and New York: A. S. Barnes, 1971; London: Thomas Yoseloff 1971.

Chaplin's first year in films seen in this fully illustrated account of Keystone's total work.

McCaffrey, Donald W. *Four Great Comedians: Chaplin, Lloyd, Keaton, Langdon*. London: Tantivy Press; New York: A. S. Barnes, 1968.

> An analysis, more sharply critical than usual, of Chaplin as filmmaker.

————, ed. *Focus on Chaplin*. New Jersey: Prentice Hall, 1971.

> An indispensable collection of quotations, essays and reviews relating to Chaplin's whole career. Useful and comprehensive bibliography.

McDonald, Gerald D., and others. *The Films of Charlie Chaplin*. New York: Citadel, 1965.

> Chaplin's films, illustrated lavishly with stills. The plots of the films are outlined, and reviews are quoted.

Minney, R. J. *Chaplin, The Immortal Tramp*. London: G. Newnes, 1954.

> A personal study of Chaplin and his work by a friend of the family.

Montgomery, John. *Comedy Films*. London: George Allen and Unwin, 1954.

> Chaplin's work seen in the context of a general history of comic filmmaking.

Payne, Robert. *The Great God Pan: A Biography of the Tramp Played by Charlie Chaplin*. New York: Hermitage House, 1952

> A sometimes imaginative, often rather farfetched and fanciful study of the significance of Chaplin's work.

Quigley, Isabel. *Charlie Chaplin; Early Comedies*. London: Studio Vista, 1968.

> A splendidly illustrated account of the films up to 1919, with an analytical essay.

Robinson, David. *The Great Funnies: A History of Film Comedy*. London: Studio Vista, 1969.

> An outline history of the work of the great comedians by one of Britain's most sympathetic and informed critics.

Sennett, Mack, and Shipp, Cameron. *King of Comedy*. New York: Doubleday, 1954; London: Peter Davies, 1955.

    A highly entertaining account of the early days at Keystone, to be taken as a record of the spirit more than the fact.

Tyler, Parker. *Chaplin: Last of the Clowns*. New York: Vanguard Press, 1947.

    A perceptive, if at moments somewhat pretentious analysis of Chaplin and his work.

Index